ASSESSING INDIVIDUAL NEEDS

A Practical Approach

Second Edition

HARRY AYERS
DON CLARKE
ALASTAIR ROSS

David Fulton Publishers
London

David Fulton Publishers Ltd
Ormond House, 26–27 Boswell Street, London WC1N 3JD
Web site: http://www.fultonbooks.co.uk

First published in Great Britain by
David Fulton Publishers 1993

Second Edition 1996
Reprinted 1996, 1998, 1999, 2000.

Note: The right of the author to be identified as the author of this work has been asserted by him in accordance with the Copyright, Designs and Patents Act 1988.

British Library Cataloguing in Publication Data
A catalogue record for this book is available from the British Library

ISBN 1–85346–440–6

Typeset by Don Clarke
Printed in Great Britain by Bell and Bain Ltd, Glasgow

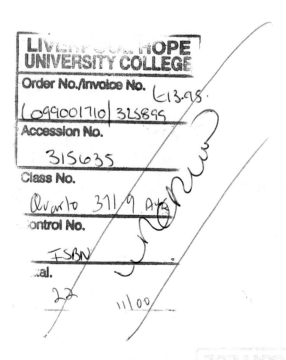

Contents

Acknowledgements

The original version of this book was designed and prepared by a group of teachers who worked at the Tower Hamlets Schools Support Team partly as a result of funding through the Elton Support Grant.

This version of **Assessing Individual Needs** was designed and written by *Harry Ayers, Don Clarke and Alastair Ross*

We would like to thank the following people:

Francesca Gray – for her contribution to the design of the IEP forms

Sue Aldridge – for her contribution to the design of the Literacy IEP

We would also like to acknowledge the contribution made by *Martin Bonathan* (now SEN Policy Advisor, Birmingham LEA) to the original version.

Harry Ayers, Don Clarke, Alastair Ross, Francesca Gray and Sue Aldridge are teachers in the *Tower Hamlets Support for Learning Service.*

Preface

This handbook is a guide for **all** teachers in assessing the individual needs of pupils in primary and secondary schools but will be of particular use to Special Educational Needs Co-ordinators.

The accompanying profiles and forms are designed to enable teachers to summarise and collate their perceptions of pupils with the aim of contributing to the process of determining the needs of pupils who are causing concern. We hope this will make it possible to think more clearly about how those needs are being met in the classroom and, more broadly, within the school. The profiles and forms can also be used by pastoral heads, SEN teachers and departments. Since the **SEN Code of Practice** has been introduced schools have a statutory duty to record SEN information about pupils and to produce **Individual Education Plans (IEPs)**. The aim of this book is to assist teachers to contribute to that process in a focussed manner. Two key SEN areas are **Behaviour** and **Literacy**. **Two IEP forms** focussing on those areas are included in the book along with explanatory notes. Also included are a variety of observation sheets and means for recording information about pupils.

1. Introducing the Profiles

This chapter introduces the Pupil Assessment Profile which comes in both Primary and Secondary versions.

The contents of this chapter include the following:

- *Introduction to the the profiles*

- *An example profile*

- *Reasons why teachers should use the profiles*

- *How behaviour and learning can be measured*

THE PROFILES

The profiles are a means of recording and collating teachers' perceptions of primary and secondary school pupils.

They encourage teachers to structure their perceptions using specific behavioural and learning categories.

They also enable teachers to rank those perceptions along continua under the different categories.

Properly used these profiles will encourage teachers to be systematic, consistent and comprehensive in their perceptions of pupils.

Finally these profiles are not 'scientific' instruments in the psychometric sense but are based on teachers' perceptions which have to form the basis for any action plan or intervention involving pupils.

Secondary Assessment Profile

Pupil [   ]   Form [   ]   N C Year [   ]   Date [   ]

Form Tutor [   ]   Gender: **M / F**   Subject [   ]

Home Language [   ]   E2L Stage: **1 2 3 4**   Medical [   ]

On each continuum, circle the appropriate number. When indicating behaviour consider only the last 6 weeks. Underline example words which you think are appropriate, adding others which you think describe the pupil's difficulties or achievements

Average or Acceptable
↓
Concern → 1 2 3 4 5 ← Excellent

1) Attendance [   ] % age   1 2 3 4 5   **2) Punctuality**   1 2 3 4 5

LEARNING / WORK
Fill in Attainment Targets as appropriate

AT 1   Level or KS [   ]   AT 2   Level or KS [   ]

AT 3   Level or KS [   ]   AT 4   Level or KS [   ]

General comments about subject:
Do these results reflect the pupil's potential?

3) Standard of work

4) Starting work
Needs to have things very clearly explained
Frequently finds an excuse / Has to be prompted to
Wants to do something different

6) Working cooperatively
Chats a lot / Dominates   Fails to work with others
Finds it difficult to share

8) Organisational skills
Loses work / Fails to bring equipment

Primary Assessment Profile

Pupil [   ]   N C Year [   ]   Date [   ]

Class [   ]   E2L Stage: **1 2 3 4**   Home Language [   ]

Gender: **M / F**   Medical [   ]   Teacher [   ]

On each continuum, circle the appropriate number. When indicating behaviour consider only the last 6 weeks. Underline example words which you think are appropriate, adding others which you think describe the pupil's difficulties or achievements

Average or Acceptable
↓
Concern → 1 2 3 4 5 ← Excellent

1) Attendance [   ] % age   1 2 3 4 5

2) Punctuality   1 2 3 4 5

LEARNING / WORK
English
1) Speaking and Listening   Level [   ]
2) Reading   Level [   ]
3) Writing   Level [   ]

Mathematics
1) Using and Applying Maths   Level [   ]
2) Number and Algebra   Level [   ]
3) Shape, Space and Measuring   Level [   ]
4) Handling Data   Level [   ]

Science
1) Experimental and Investigative Science   Level [   ]
2) Life processes and Living Things   Level [   ]
3) Materials and Properties   Level [   ]
4) Physical Processes   Level [   ]

Do these results reflect the pupil's potential?

Comments on other subject areas:
(Indicate levels of subjects which are below or above average)

3) Starting work   1 2 3 4 5
Needs to have things very clearly explained
Frequently finds an excuse / Has to be prompted to start
Wants to do something different

4) Working cooperatively   1 2 3 4 5
Chats a lot / Dominates / Fails to work with others
Finds it difficult to share

5) Work   1 2 3 4 5
Work usually unfinished / Badly presented
Only finishes work if kept in / Lack of care or pride
Destroys own work / Easily becomes discouraged
Copies other people / Seems satisfied with very little

6) Organisational skills   1 2 3 4 5
Loses work / Fails to bring equipment

7) Working independently   1 2 3 4 5
Always asking for help
Fails to work on own
Gets on well by themselves

8) Managing difficulties in work   1 2 3 4 5
Quickly gets frustrated / Gives up / Avoids work
Needs a lot of reassurance and help
Finds it difficult to remember things
Finds it difficult to concentrate

REASONS WHY TEACHERS SHOULD USE THESE PROFILES

There are two kinds of profiles:

Primary and Secondary (each one on an A4 sheet).

These profiles are specially designed for use in primary and secondary schools. They have been piloted in schools and as a result the format and text are based on teachers' suggestions.

The profiles are comprehensive in that they cover all aspects of a pupil's behaviour and learning relating to a primary or secondary school.

The profiles are very easy to understand and use. They are visually attractive and can be rapidly scanned and assimilated by the teacher. TIME TAKEN TO COMPLETE IS MINIMAL.

The **secondary version has a score sheet** (also on an A4 sheet) which makes it easy for the person responsible to collate the information in a visual format.

There are a range of uses for the profiles depending on the aims of the teacher and the school.

They can be used as baselines for judging trends in the behaviour and learning of a pupil. They can show the longitudinal development of a pupil's learning and behaviour. The secondary version allows cross-sectional comparisons of a pupil's behaviour and learning relating them to both subjects and categories. Most importantly they can be used in the **preparation and evaluation of IEPs**. They are also useful as "round robins" for referral and highlighting meetings.

In practice we have found that because the forms are easy to fill in there is a high return rate and that forms tend to be returned quickly. The result is that information gathered on pupils is comprehensive.

THESE PROFILES ENABLE TEACHERS AND SCHOOLS TO HAVE
UP-TO-DATE AND FULL INFORMATION ON PUPILS WITH MINIMAL EFFORT.

8

HOW CAN WE MEASURE BEHAVIOUR AND LEARNING?

A pupil's behaviour and learning can be measured through observation. This observation can be undertaken by the class teacher or by an independent observer.

Observation can be formal or informal or a mixture of both.

Formal observation is where the observer uses an instrument or schedule that enables that observer to fill in or tick off the frequency and duration of discrete categories of behaviour. Alternatively a specific type of behaviour can be inserted for a particular period of time .

Informal observation occurs where an observer scans a pupil's behaviour in a setting without using an instrument or schedule. The observer records observations as they are perceived and this could be at random or systematically (see **ABC Sheets**).

The observer can use different types of observation instruments i.e. those that sample time and those that sample events. Time sampling is where particular behaviours are recorded over a particular time interval (See **Fixed Interval Sheet**). Event sampling is where a particular event is recorded in terms of its frequency (see **Frequency Count Sheet**).

The purpose of measuring a pupil's behaviour and learning is to enable a baseline to be established which will lead to a more reliable evaluation of progress. This information can be plotted on a chart enabling a teacher to have a visual display of a pupil's progress over time.

Interventions with pupils can be evaluated by establishing baselines and then observing pupils at different points during interventions to assess progress. The sheets are particularly useful evidence for **IEPs**.

The **Pupil Assessment Profiles** can guide teachers in terms of what categories to use in the process of observing pupils. This will encourage a systematic approach to observing behaviour and learning. The scoresheets can in turn be used to summarise teachers' observations and serve as baseline data for future comparison of a pupil's behaviour and learning.

2. Using the Assessment Profiles

When to use the profile:

IN THE PRIMARY SCHOOL

The **Primary Assessment Profile (PAP)** is designed to be a part of the primary teacher's own monitoring and assessment procedures where a pupil is giving cause for concern. More formally, the Primary Assessment Profile could well be included as part of the information gathering aspect of Stage 1 of the **SEN Code of Practice**. The form can also be used to formalise information about the child at SEN Stages 2 and beyond as it is a convenient way of setting and monitoring baselines of behaviour and learning.

Stage 1 of the Code of Practice indicates that the class teacher will gather information about the child causing concern. Stage 2/3 involves the drawing up of an **Individual Education Plan (IEP)** in conjunction with the Special Educational Needs Coordinator (SENCO). SENCOs will find the Primary Assessment Profile a helpful way of maintaining a degree of consistency in this process between different classrooms.

At Stage 3, when external agencies are involved in the drawing up of IEPs, the forms will provide a concise resumé of information about a pupil. This is discussed further in Chapter 6.

IN THE SECONDARY SCHOOL

The **Secondary Assessment Profile (SAP)** is designed to be a part of the secondary school's own monitoring and assessment procedures where a pupil is giving cause for concern. Form tutors and subject teachers already through their classroom and school based informal observation will have judged the pupil's behaviour and/or learning as problematic. This judgement will have been supported by relevant teachers' and school records.

The Head of Year, or other person responsible for an overview of a pupil's education, can issue the secondary profile form to all the pupil's subject teachers as well as the form tutor in order to focus the teachers' observations of the pupil in a systematic way. Alternatively, forms may be issued by the SENCO as described in Chapter 6.

Secondary Assessment Profile

Pupil	*Jason*	Form **8 DC**	N C Year **8**	Date **1.12.95**

Form Tutor *Mr Clarke*   Gender: **M / F**   Subject *Maths*

Home Language [ ]   E2L Stage: *1 2 3 4*   Medical [ ]

On each continuum, circle the appropriate number. When indicating behaviour consider only the last 6 weeks. Underline example words which you think are appropriate, adding others which you think describe the pupil's difficulties or achievements

Average or Acceptable
↓
Concern → 1 2 **3** 4 5 ← Excellent

1) Attendance [ ] % age   1 2 3 ④ 5   **2) Punctuality**   1 ② 3 4 5

LEARNING / WORK
Fill in Attainment Targets as appropriate

AT 1 *Using + applying* Level or KS **2**   AT 2 *Number/Algebra* Level or KS **4**

AT 3 *Shape/Space/M's.* Level or KS **3**   AT 4 *Data Handling* Level or KS **1**

General comments about subject:
Do these results reflect the pupil's potential? *Yes. Jason still has difficulty grasping the basic operations. He is quite confident about positive whole numbers. + Place value .1 → 0.9*

3) Standard of work   1 ② 3 4 5

4) Starting work   ① 2 3 4 5
Needs to have things very clearly explained
Frequently finds an excuse / <u>Has to be prompted to start</u>
Wants to do something different
Needs a lot of reassurance

5) Work   1 ② 3 4 5
<u>Work usually unfinished</u> / badly presented
Only finishes work if kept in / Lack of care or pride
Destroys own work / Easily becomes discouraged
Copies other people / <u>Seems satisfied with very little</u>

6) Working cooperatively   1 2 ③ 4 5
<u>Chats a lot</u> / Dominates   Fails to work with others
Finds it difficult to share

7) Working independently   1 ② 3 4 5
Always asking for help   Gets on well by themselves
Fails to work on own

8) Organisational skills   1 2 3 4 5
Loses work / Fails to bring equipment
Never seems to have a pen or ruler

9) Managing difficulties in work   ① 2 3 4 5
<u>Quickly gets frustrated</u>, <u>Gives up</u>, <u>Avoids work</u>
<u>Needs a lot of reassurance and help</u>
<u>Finds it difficult to remember things</u>
<u>Finds it difficult to concentrate</u>

Side 1 of a filled in Secondary Profile

11

How to fill in the profile

The teacher should not spend a lot of time on it, as the aim is to gain an overall impression. It is important to emphasise that this is not a scientific process, but rather a means to record staffs' perceptions of a pupil which can then be used as a basis for further, more focussed observation and assessment if it is considered necessary.

The Sections:

There are 7 sections to complete:

The 1st Section: General pupil information

The 2nd Section: Punctuality and Attendance (1 – 2)

The 3rd Section: National Curriculum Levels of Achievement

The 4th Section: Learning and Work (3 – 10)

The 5th Section: Personal and Social (11 – 18)

The 6th section: Behaviour (19 – 24)

The 7th Section: Summary

The numbered sections are usually comprised of three parts:

i)   A continuum, 1 – 5 where:

      1 Can be indicates POOR or EXTREMELY UNSATISFACTORY.

      3 Indicates AVERAGE or REASONABLY ACCEPTABLE

      5 Indicates EXCELLENT or EXTREMELY SATISFACTORY

      It is intended that teachers circle an appropriate number on each continuum where they "feel" the pupil to generally be. It is worth trying to remember how the pupil has been over the previous month or six weeks. General behaviour patterns rather Isolated incidents or difficulties should form the basis of this rough assessment.

ii)   A series of prompt words and phrases. These can be underlined by the teacher to amplify or clarify either positives or negatives.

iii) A space is available for the teacher to add further comment, should they wish.

The 1st Section: *General Pupil Information*

Primary Assessment Profile

Pupil		N C Year [ ] Date [ ][ ][ ]
Class [ ] E2L Stage: *1 2 3 4*	Home Language [ ]
Gender: *M / F* Medical [ ]	Teacher [ ]

This section is for the teacher to complete with general pupil information. If English is not the pupil's mother tongue there is space to indicate the their grasp of the English language as well as space to indicate the language spoken in their home. In a secondary school this kind of information may not be available to all staff and could well be determined by the SENCO.

There is also a box to indicate whether or not there are significant medical concerns which staff should be aware of.

Secondary Assessment Profile

Pupil [ ]	Form [ ] N C Year [ ] Date [ ]
Form Tutor [ ]	Gender: *M / F* Subject [ ]
Home Language [ ]	E2L Stage: *1 2 3 4* Medical [ ]

There are minor differences between the primary and secondary forms.

The 2nd Section: *Attendance and Punctuality*

1) Attendance [ ] % age *1 2 3 4 5*	**2) Punctuality** *1 2 3 4 5*

This section allows the teacher to record either a general impression of these areas or a precise percentage. In a secondary school the form tutor could record the pupil's attendance at school rather than for a specific subject area.

The 3rd Section: *National Curriculum Levels of Achievement*

Attendance ___ % age   1 2 3 4 5

Punctuality   1 2 3 4 5

ENGLISH
1) Speaking and Listening   Level ☐
2) Reading   Level ☐
3) Writing   Level ☐

MATHEMATICS
1) Using and Applying Maths   Level ☐
2) Number and Algebra   Level ☐
3) Shape, Space and Measuring   Level ☐
4) Handling Data   Level ☐

SCIENCE
1) Experimental and Investigative Science   Level ☐
2) Life processes and Living Things   Level ☐
3) Materials and Properties   Level ☐
4) Physical Processes   Level ☐

Do these results reflect the pupil's potential?

Comments on other subject areas:
(Indicate levels of subjects which are below or above average:)

The primary version of the form has separate areas for the three core subjects of the National Curriculum – English, Mathematics and Science. The teacher is then encouraged to note whether these measurements fit with their personal assessment of the pupil. Space is also given to allow for comments on other subject areas. These should include both strengths and weaknesses, likes and dislikes.

The secondary version allows for each subject teacher to indicate the level at which the pupil works within their subject. General comments can also be added.

LEARNING / WORK
Fill in Attainment Targets as appropriate

AT 1   Level or KS ☐   **AT 2**   Level or KS ☐

AT 3   Level or KS ☐   **AT 4**   Level or KS ☐

General comments about subject:
Do these results reflect the pupil's potential?

The 4th Section: Learning and Work

The aim of this section is to record how the pupil approaches their work in a variety of settings. **Items 3,4 and 5** focus on the process of work.

Items 6 and 7 focus on the pupil's ability to work independently. A low score here would perhaps suggest that the pupil constantly requires reassurance from the teacher. Specific concerns can be recorded below each item.

Item 8 focuses on the pupil's ability to organise themselves. This might include the organisation of materials and equipment, work or even being in the right place at the right time. Can they keep a track of their work or does it always seem to get 'lost'? Do they never have a pencil or ruler? Do they always have excuses for not having homework?

Item 9 focuses on the pupil's response to difficulties that arise in the progress of work. Do they 'give up'? Do they become demanding of teacher's attention or disruptive of other pupil's work? Some pupils who experience frustration with work will get themselves excluded from the classroom (by misbehaving) in order to avoid the discomfort of the frustration and sense of failure.

---

3) Standard of work   *1 2 3 4 5*

4) Starting work   *1 2 3 4 5*
Needs to have things very clearly explained
Frequently finds an excuse / Has to be prompted to start
Wants to do something different

5) Work   *1 2 3 4 5*
Work usually unfinished / badly presented
Only finishes work if kept in / Lack of care or pride
Destroys own work / Easily becomes discouraged
Copies other people / Seems satisfied with very little

6) Working cooperatively   *1 2 3 4 5*
Chats a lot / Dominates   Fails to work with others
Finds it difficult to share

7) Working independently   *1 2 3 4 5*
Always asking for help   Gets on well by themselves
Fails to work on own

8) Organisational skills   *1 2 3 4 5*
Loses work / Fails to bring equipment

9) Managing difficulties in work   *1 2 3 4 5*
Quickly gets frustrated, Gives up, Avoids work
Needs a lot of reassurance and help
Finds it difficult to remember things
Finds it difficult to concentrate

The 5th Section: Personal and Social

PERSONAL and SOCIAL

10) Self-confidence   1 2 3 4 5
Copes with difficulties, appears worried   Recognises own successes
Over-reacts to events   Can be given responsibilities
Demands attention

11) Awareness of other's needs 1 2 3 4 5
Seems only concerned about themselves   Can listen to others
Inappropriate helpfulness   Helpful to staff, helpful to peers
Shows insight into others' situations

12) Self-awareness   1 2 3 4 5
Can discuss difficulties   Can express feelings appropriately
Reacts defensively
Doesn't seem to take responsibility for own actions

13) Following instructions   1 2 3 4 5
Unable to follow simple instructions
Able to follow complicated instructions
Frequently needs reassurance

14) Friendship   1 2 3 4 5
Has few friends   Has lots of friends
Fails to make positive contact   Tries to be 'helpful'
Tends to follow, Dominates others

15) Responding to correction   1 2 3 4 5
Over-reacts   Responds well and changes behaviour
Accepts correction with difficulty

16) Managing disagreements   1 2 3 4 5
Gets into lots of disagreements
Disagreements often end in a fight

17) Managing in the playground 1 2 3 4 5
Finds it difficult to join in   Plays well with others
Gets picked on, Bullied

These items are concerned with:

- *the way the child is able to manage themselves and their feelings*

- *other people and their feelings*

- *managing particular social situations, with peers and with staff*

Two key skills linked to difficult behaviour are:

- *the ability to manage one's own painful feelings, particularly anger*

- *social skills related to full participation in school life*

The school may need to consider whether it is offering opportunities for pupils to learn these skills. Some basic skills have not been learnt by some pupils and very direct teaching of these skills can be necessary. More generally, how the school addresses the 'affective curriculum' – the way feelings affect pupils' ability to learn and participate in school life may also need to be considered through, for example, the academic curriculum, circle work or assertiveness skills training.

Some schools provide training for their pupils in conflict resolution, use of peer-mediation and peer-counselling skills. See a later section for a description of a model for conflict resolution used in a primary school.

In using this assessment profile it is important to link up observations of a pupil's behaviour with those relating to social / personal skills and learning.

The 6th Section: Behaviour

BEHAVIOUR

18) Interactions with peers   *1 2 3 4 5*
Physically aggressive, verbally aggressive
Works well with others, Finds it difficult to join in
Gets picked on, Bullied

19) Interactions with adults   *1 2 3 4 5*
Physically aggressive, verbally aggressive
Withdrawn, Provoking, Attention demanding

20) Use of equipment   *1 2 3 4 5*
Misuse of equipment, furnature or materials
Minor vandalism, Major vandalism

21) Pupil noise   *1 2 3 4 5*
Constant talking to peers, Shouting out
Interrupting teacher, Non-verbal noises
Banging, or tapping

22) Movement about the class   *1 2 3 4 5*
Wandering about, moving around on the mat
Interferring with others, Leaving the room
Going to the toilet wiithout permission

23) Public areas   *1 2 3 4 5*
Corridors, Playground, Assembly, Toilets, Office
Physical / Verbal aggression to staff / pupils
Intentional / unintentional interference of others
Noise, Misuse of equipment, Graffiti, Litter

24) How does the pupil's behaviour compare with others in the class?

Much worse	*Worse*	*Average*	*Better*	*Much Better*
1	*2*	*3*	*4*	*5*

These items focus on the pupil's perceived behaviour and cover the usual areas of difficulty. When describing a pupil's behaviour it is important to be as objective and descriptive as possible.

Section 24 enables a teacher to record how the pupils behaviour compares with the rest of the class. A temptation when working towards improvement in a pupil's behaviour is to expect them to be better than everybody else. A fair goal is to be average. After that, the goal should be an improvement in the behaviour of the class as a whole.

Please indicate the two areas that you are most concerned about:

Please indicate any areas of strength or improvements made recently:

Please indicate any strategies you have found useful:

17

The 7th Section: Summary

One key strategy in planning for a change in behaviour is prioritising one or two goals so that the whole project becomes achievable. Probably the most important change that has to take place is for the pupil (and perhaps staff) to believe that any change can take place. As part of this, noting down any positives begins to shift the balance in the right direction. This is important:

a)   to achieve as balanced a view of the child as possible

b)   to locate points of positive contact in either work or relationships on which to build. For an intervention to work, it is probably essential for the teacher to have in their mind the strengths of the child so as to be able to offset the child's own negative view of themselves which is often apparent in children with learning and behaviour difficulties.

Moving on

The next steps are to:

*   For secondary schools, to fill out the score sheets

*   Go through the PLANNING process and work towards deciding on an intervention.

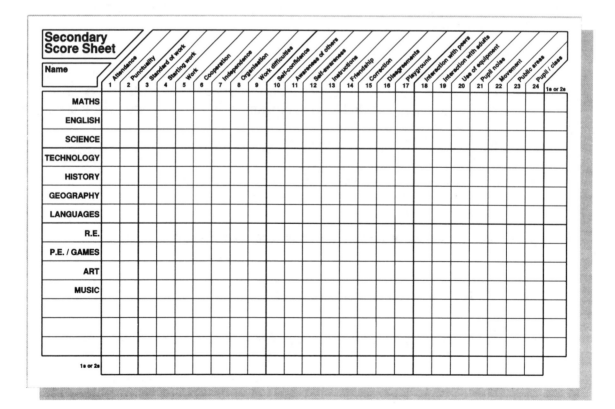

Scoring the Secondary Profile

This score sheet enables a class tutor, Head of House or Year etc to collate and compare the scores from all the SAPs completed by all the subject teachers. The scores from the individual subjects can be inserted on the score sheet by the subject teachers themselves or by the Head of Year or House or the Class tutor. The scores inserted will range from 1 to 5. The teacher responsible will simply copy the scores from the SAPs onto the appropriate cells for the 20 categories alongside the designated subjects.

Secondary Score Sheet

Name	Attendance 1	Punctuality 2	Standard of work 3	Starting work 4	Work 5	Cooperation 6	Independenc 7	Org 8
MATHS	5	5	4	2	5	3	2	3
ENGLISH	3	3	2	3	1	3	3	4
SCIENCE	4	3	1	3	2	3	3	3
TECHNOLOGY	3	3	2	3	2	4	4	3
HISTORY	2	2	1	3	2	2	3	3

Teachers find it useful if 1s and 2s are highlighted to pick out underlying patterns. In the above example it can be seen that the pupil is of great concern in **History** as well has having difficulty in **Standard of Work** and **Work** across most of the subjects. It also looks likely that he seems quite keen on **Maths** but finds it difficult to work independently.

The score sheet enables teachers to establish a baseline from which it is possible at selected intervals to see how a pupil is perceived to be performing in the 24 different categories and in the different subject areas. It should be possible for teachers to see if there has been any perceived improvement or deterioration in the pupil's behaviour or learning. This can be achieved by comparing successive score sheets over a period of time.

3. Observation

DEFINITION:

Direct observation refers to the recording of overt behaviour of pupils in a variety of contexts e.g. classrooms and playgrounds. This recording can be achieved through both natural and artificial means i.e. by the human senses or by the use of video equipment. It enables an observer to acquire an idea of the FREQUENCY, INTENSITY, LATENCY and DURATION of events. Observation from the behavioural perspective requires the recording of OVERT, SPECIFIC and DISCRETE events or actions e.g. seeing and recording the throwing of a ruler or swearing at a teacher. It is advisable for there to be agreement among those involved on what constitutes a particular event or action.

IMPORTANCE:

Direct observation forms an important part of the whole assessment procedure. It is advantageous where pupils display limited verbal skills or where they are reluctant to communicate with adults. The use of observation also increases objectivity and requires a lower level of inference than some other forms of assessment. Through direct observation a BASELINE can be constructed. This baseline consists of a count of specific and overt behaviours e.g. the number of times a pupil leaves their seat. By establishing a baseline it is possible to evaluate the effectiveness of an intervention by comparing the results of the intervention with the pre-intervention baseline.

Direct observation enables a FUNCTIONAL or ABC ANALYSIS to be undertaken. This involves observing a pupil to see what happens before (the ANTECEDENTS) and after (the CONSEQUENCES) a particular pupil's problem BEHAVIOUR (B). From this analysis it may be possible to bring about positive behavioural change by altering the antecedents or consequences of the problem behaviour.

TYPES:

Informal observation consists of making notes of the pupil's behaviours without quantifying or counting them.

Formal observation consists of using an observation schedule that enables the observer to quantify the pupil's behaviours.

CONTEXTS:

Direct observation can be undertaken in many different contexts but can be very difficult in those contexts where the pupil is constantly moving e.g. in the playground.

PROCEDURES:

Before observing it is necessary to consider the following questions:

Has permission been sought for observation of the pupil?

What are the specific problem behaviours?

Have the behaviours been objectively i.e. precisely defined?

When and where do the behaviours occur?

Do the behaviours occur in one or more contexts?

Have you avoided being identified as observing the pupil?

Have you encouraged the teacher to proceed as usual when taking the class?

Have you established an observing position that allows an unrestricted view?

METHODS AND EQUIPMENT:

There are different methods of recording observations:

Frequency recording:

A record is made of the number of times a given behaviour occurs within a chosen period of time. This kind of recording depends on the behaviour being discrete, having a reasonable duration and with not too high a frequency.

Duration recording:

A record is made of the amount of time the pupil is engaged in the behaviour or the length of time between the commencement of observation and the beginning of the behaviour. Again the behaviours should be discrete and have a reasonable duration.

Interval recording:

This method consists in recording the presence or absence of behaviours in a series of equal time slots

CONDITIONS:

Objective definitions of behaviour:

It is useful to define a pupil's behaviour in OBSERVABLE and SPECIFIC terms so as to avoid subjectivity. The idea is that all observers would then be able to agree on the occurrence or non-occurrence of a particular behaviour. The definition should be precise enough to avoid vagueness. Objectivity can enable discussions about a pupil's behaviour to be freer from ambiguities and idiosyncratic judgments. Teachers can then be more certain that they are talking about the same problem behaviours.

General vs. specific descriptions of behaviour:

Where possible it is desirable to break down general behavioural descriptions into more specific descriptions e.g. physical aggression-where a pupil hits another pupil causing that pupil to cry out in pain.

PROBLEMS:

Reactivity

This problem arises where the pupil is aware that they are being observed and behaves differently during the observation period. When this happens the pupil's behaviour usually improves whilst under observation. This problem usually disappears after the pupil has become accustomed to being observed. The pupil then reverts to their usual behaviour.

High Level of inference

This problem can arise due to the observer going beyond what is strictly observed and making unwarranted statements about the pupil's behaviour.

Observer bias

This problem can arise from differences in how observers define behaviours, how they record their observations and whether they maintain reliability over time. Inter-rater reliability is necessary so as to avoid observers recording the same events differently.

Insufficient observation

This problem arises where there have been an insufficient number of observations of the pupil's behaviours. Insufficient observations adversely affect their validity and reliability. It is impossible to state what the ideal number of observations are due to time and cost constraints but it is advisable to undertake as many as possible.

Inter-rater reliability

Ideally observers should agree on definitions of specific kinds of behaviour and also agree on methods of recording those behaviours. In order for this to occur observers need to practise together. This should result in observers recording the same observations on the same pupil at the same time. This process helps to avoid the problem of subjectivity where different observers observing the same behaviour arrive at different conclusions. From time to time it is necessary for observers to check that they still agree with each others observations. This is to avoid observer drift, a process whereby observers over a period of time drift away from agreed definitions and recording methods.

Some basic principles of observation

Preparation

It is extremely important to prepare carefully for an observation. The teacher should know in advance that the observation will be taking place. She may also wish to inform the class that someone will be sitting in on the lesson although not specifying the exact purpose of the visitor. It depends very much on the ethos of the school whether another adult sitting in a classroom constitutes an unusual event. In any case, children very quickly ignore the observer, particularly if they do not engage unduly in conversations with them.

The nature and content of the lesson should also be known in advance and noted as part of the observation. It is helpful to get some understanding of the teacher's intentions as this will provide a context for analysing the information afterwards. It may be possible, also, to identify particular activities within an overall period through a FIS if the overall lesson plan is understood.

The observer should have any materials or equipment, usually a clipboard, stopwatch, paper, pencil / pen, observation schedule ready and to hand.

They should find a place in the classroom which is unobtrusive but which allows them to see and hear the individual being observed clearly enough. In primary classrooms this is not always easy as the class may be moving around or switching activities. Be prepared to move but with care!

Timing

Since the observation will be used to verify or clarify the results of the Pupil Assessment Profile it will be important to target the observations at particular activities or academic areas for them to have any useful function in providing more precise information. The PAP should highlight areas of difficulty which can then be targeted for particular observations although discussion with the teacher beforehand are also important in targeting these areas.

Frequency

The frequency of observations will depend on various factors. Probably the most important factor will be the amount of time available to do observations and in these times this may be overriding. However it is important that the observations relate to the identified problem/s and this may entail observing different settings in order to establish some means of comparison. Also, it is sometimes not enough to observe a particular activity once, since the behaviour of the identified pupil may not be typical and the only way is to observe over a period of time.

As we said before, sometimes a pupil may pick up that they are being observed and adjust their behaviour but in such cases, particularly with younger pupils, they usually return quickly to their usual patterns of behaviour.

Fixed Interval Sampling

The Fixed Interval Sampling (FIS) is a type of observation schedule which can be used by anyone after a brief amount of instruction. It sorts off-task behaviour into a series of categories which are assigned a particular code. The observer notes the predominant behaviour of the pupil for each 15 second interval of a total period of time which could extend up to twenty or thirty minutes, depending on the activity. In practice, this is usually done by observing for 10 seconds and recording for 5.

At the end of the observation it is possible to calculate the different proportions of each category of behaviour noted during the total period of observation. By also writing, for instance, a T in a cell when the teacher and pupil are interacting it is also possible to record the amount of personal attention the pupil receives. If another symbol is also used, eg a P, it is also possible to record whether the interactions are pupil or teacher initiated. Similarly, using appropriate symbols, the balance of positive and negative, task-based and off-task interactions can be recorded if deemed useful.

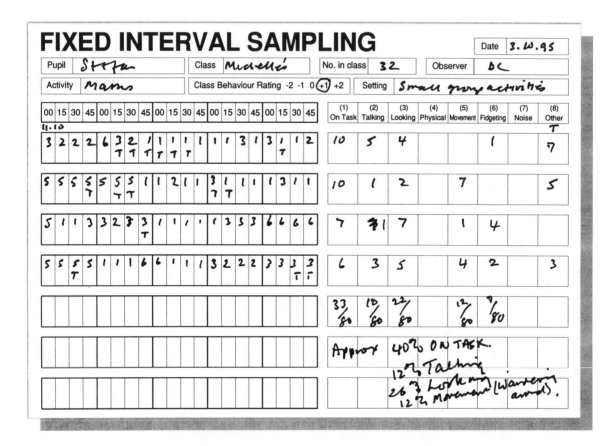

The Fixed Interval Sampling Sheet

The ABC Form

Once observations have been conducted it is helpful to look at the accumulated information in a more analytical way. The ABC sheet enables teachers to collect and organise information in a way which reveals patterns of behaviour and learning in relation to three areas:

Antecedents: the setting in which the behaviour occurs, including the event or events which happen immediately before the behaviour

Behaviour: the behaviour itself in very clear, precise terms

Consequences: what happens afterwards, what seems to reinforce the behaviour

What is important about this sheet is the principle that behaviour / learning is related to a context and that it is only when teachers can be precise and clear about what is happening that they can actually change the pattern through some kind of intervention.

Both teachers and pupils tend to behave differently in different settings and equally they are influenced by what happens immediately or sometime before their current behaviour. Behaviour of a pupil can also be influenced by what they awarely or unawarely think is going to happen.

Through being precise about the behaviour itself it is possible to be clearer about what exactly needs to be changed.

it is important to remembers that the behaviour is likely to be repeated if the consequence of the behaviour is experienced as rewarding by the pupil. It is also important to remember that pupils can experience some 'punishments' as rewarding. For instance, being kept in at playtime (particularly on a cold day), may be experienced by the pupil as exceedingly rewarding!

This following graphic illustrates is the basic version of an ABC sheet for use in observing pupils. (It can be used by the class teacher themselves or by an observer. If the the behaviours causing concern are fairly infrequent, then the class teacher is likely to be the best person.) The particular behaviour is recorded along with the date and time. If time allows, brief details about contributing factors or contexts as well as outcomes of the behaviour can also be noted. Outcomes can include: *What happens to the pupil / How other pupils react / How staff react*

ABC of Behaviour

Date/Time	Antecedents	Behaviour	Consequences

The following sheet shows the kind of input intended for each column. Teachers might be able to think of other items which can be added. It can be helpful as part of the planning process to think about ANTECEDENTS more broadly and the following sheet has been divided into two groups: GENERAL and SPECIFIC. Specific ANTECEDENTS tend to be those that are immediate to the classroom. The General antecedents are much broader factors which may include a significant degree of conjecture.

ABC of Behaviour

Antecedents General	Antecedents Specific	Behaviour	Consequences
Home General ability in school Learning difficulties Level of self-confidence / self-esteem General standard of work Peer relationships Staff relationships Status in class Pupil's strengths/ weaknesses? Medical / physical difficulties	Where does it occur? Time if day? Kind of activity / task? What was expected of pupil? Stucture of work setting? How do you think pupil was feeling? How do think pupil perceived situation? How much positive/negative contact with teacher?	What did you actually see happen Observable and objective description of behaviour Consider frequency, severity and appropriateness	What happens afterwards? What does the pupil achieve from the behaviour? Pos Neg? How do staff react? How do other pupils react? What do they say or do? How does pupil feel? What doesn't happen or what is avoided? What view of the world might the responses reinforce?

SEN Class Monitoring Sheet:

This sheet can be used in order to identify pupils for inclusion on the school's SEN register at Stage 1. This sheet would probably cover roughly half a term and if a pupil's name appears on a regular basis – for whatever reason – it is likely that their name should be entered into the SEN register or at least raised at a 'highlighting' or 'cause for concern' meeting.

A primary teacher would aim to spend a few minutes at the end of each week going through their class in their mind and indicating on the sheet particular concerns (or positives). It is quite likely that most children will usually not warrant a mention.

In secondary school a subject teacher may only use it to monitor pupils who have provoked some concern.

The areas indicated here are some that have been in use in one particular school and can be varied to suit particular circumstances. More than one category can be indicated.

SEN Class Monitoring Sheet

Date / Name	2/4	9/4	16/4	23/4			
Anwar	B	B		B			
Alex			V				
Michelle							
Nazmi	PR Ph		P	P			
Nazia				H			
Robbie		W V		V Wd			

B - Behaviour W - Work / Learning Ab - Absenteeism
Wd - Withdrawn H - High achievement I - Improvement
E2L Ph - Physical N - Neglect V - Visual P - Playground
PR - Pupil Relationships SR - Staff Relationships Au - Aural

4. Effective Intervention

This chapter looks at the criteria for effective interventions with primary and secondary pupils under the following headings.

A   Different types of interventions

B   Levels of intervention

C   Intervention factors

D   Targeting behaviour

E   Timing and reviewing interventions

F   Pupil involvement in interventions

G   Implementation

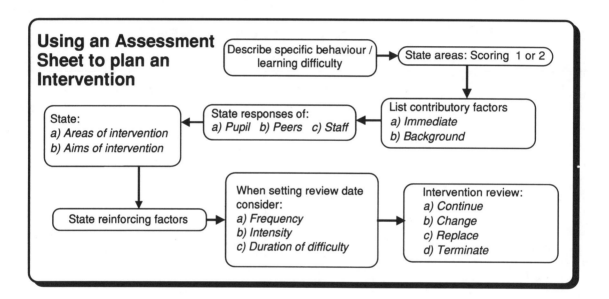

A. Different Types Of Interventions

The following interventions have been used effectively in primary and secondary schools.

OBSERVATION WITH FEEDBACK

A teacher can observe individuals, groups or classes with a view to recording teacher-pupil and pupil-pupil interactions. This information can be fed back to the class teacher and pupils with the aim of increasing mutual understanding of their relationships in the classroom. This in itself can enable teachers to improve their classroom strategies as well as positively affecting pupils' behaviours.

IN-CLASS SUPPORT

A teacher can provide in-class support for a pupil or a group. The teacher helps the pupil(s) with the organization of their work and encourages positive pupil behaviour at appropriate times. There are many ways of providing learning support in the classroom, in partnership with class teachers. Discussing these in detail is beyond the scope of this book.

WITHDRAWING THE PUPIL FROM CLASS

A teacher withdraws the pupil(s) when it appears that this would be beneficial for the following reasons:

- Avoids disrupting classroom routines.
- Allows for greater concentration on the pupil(s) problems.
- Where a confidentiality issue arises.
- Helps the pupil(s) with particularly difficult work.

BEHAVIOURAL COUNSELLING

This kind of counselling focuses on a pupil's specific, current, overt, problem behaviours in school contexts. The counsellor discusses with the pupil(s) their behaviour and its antecedents and consequences. The aim is to enable the pupil(s) to understand what leads up to his or her behaviour and what might happen as a result of it. The pupil(s) can then be counselled as to what changes need to be made in their behaviours. Once this has been achieved then a behaviour programme based on reinforcement can be implemented.

PERSON (CLIENT) CENTRED COUNSELLING

This form of counselling encourages the pupil to reflect on their problems through the teacher showing empathy, unconditional regard and genuineness. The aim is for the pupil to develop insight into their problems and to find solutions from within their own personal resources.

BEHAVIOURAL PROGRAMME

A behavioural programme is a tailor-made action plan designed to help a pupil to improve their behaviour. It can include any of the following: contracts, report cards, rewards and sanctions. It entails the pupil performing target behaviours within a framework of rewards and sanctions.

MONITORING PROGRAMME

A monitoring programme is an action-plan designed to discover how a pupil is progressing in terms of changing their behaviour. Various recording methods and instruments can be used, in particular the Pupil Assessment Profiles.

SOCIAL SKILLS TRAINING

Pupils can be placed on a social skills training programme where those pupils lack necessary interpersonal skills. The pupils are placed in a small group where such skills can be modelled and practised.

REFERRAL TO OTHER AGENCIES

Where schools have been through the appropriate Warnock stages and a pupil is still presenting problems then the school will need to refer to an external agency. In many instances this agency will be the Educational Psychology Service.

HOME VISIT

Where the pupil's problem behaviour suggests the relevance of home factors then a home visit would be useful. These factors could include: parental discord and absence, sibling rivalry, physical and sexual abuse, emotional neglect, material deprivation. Home visits are also necessary for the purposes of keeping parents informed and for eliciting and maintaining their support.

B. Levels Of Intervention

PUPIL

Many interventions are directed at the individual pupil in order to focus solely on the particular needs of that pupil. This enables the teacher to devote all their efforts on meeting the needs of that pupil.

GROUP

Some interventions will involve a group of pupils. At one level these groups will be formed as a means of improving the social skills of pupils. The composition of such groups has to be carefully controlled through attention to pupil characteristics such as: specific behaviours, age, gender, ethnicity and educational attainment. The question of the use of role models should also be considered.

Another level of group intervention will be with whole classes and groups within classes. This will happen where the problems within a class are the product of the behaviour of many individual pupils within that class. In this case it will be necessary to implement a behaviour programme that encompasses the group or the whole class itself.

YEAR

At times behaviour problems can span a whole year group. This can be particularly true of years 8 and 9. The focus will be on problems that teachers as a whole find difficult. There should be a forum where teachers can agree on a consistent approach to those problems and the appropriate interventions.

WHOLE SCHOOL

All schools need to consider the formulation, implementation and development of a whole school behaviour policy as a means of creating a unified and consistent approach among staff towards pupil behaviour.

C. Intervention Factors

REFERRAL POINT

It is necessary to consider the point at which pupils are referred . Pupils will manifest different degrees of severity in their behaviour and thereby be considered by the school as being likely to remain in school or be permanently excluded. The point at which the pupil is at will determine the effectiveness of an intervention.

ASSESSMENT

An intervention will only be as effective as the information it is based on. This information should include the following:
The pupil's specific behaviours, their intensity, frequency and duration. The contexts in which the behaviours occur. The pupil's educational attainment. The pupil's attitudes towards teachers and pupils and towards work and the whole school. The particular strategies used by the school with the pupil and their effectiveness.

ORGANISATION

School organisation should be considered in terms of how it will facilitate or impede an intervention: An effective intervention requires organisationally:
Clear and rapid inter-staff communication. Efficient methods of monitoring and recording the course of the intervention e.g. by using the Pupil Assessment Profiles. Close linkage between the aims of the intervention and their implementation. A public and private consensus among teachers as to the aims of the intervention. A way of reviewing the intervention.

CURRICULUM

An intervention may be affected by the constraints of the curriculum:
Some behaviour problems may be exacerbated by the way the curriculum is delivered. The curriculum if undifferentiated may adversely affect pupil behaviour. Some curriculum areas e.g. (Languages) may present pupils who are experiencing behaviour problems with additional difficulties.

CLASSROOM MANAGEMENT

An intervention depends crucially on the teacher's teaching style and strategies that are used in the classroom. The intervention may require the teacher to adopt or adapt particular strategies which are unacceptable to that teacher. It is desirable for the intervention to be one that the teacher can accept.

PASTORAL SYSTEM

The intervention will depend on the type of pastoral system in place in the school. Heavily punitive and confrontational systems will tend to exacerbate behaviour problems and thereby impede those interventions that depend on the consent and collaboration of the pupil.
A conducive pastoral system will be one that maintains a balance of rewards and sanctions. An emphasis on rewards is particularly productive with regard to interventions.

D. Targeting behaviour

SMART TARGETS:

Inform the pupil about teachers' expectations
Facilitate effective behavioural programmes e.g. choice of interventions
Facilitate precise monitoring and evaluation of interventions

SMART targets are ones that enable teachers to plan effective interventions:

SPECIFIC: **Refers to discrete, overt and observable behaviour** e.g. Mary should increase her time in seat by 10 minutes in the first instance. John should complete 20 addition and subtraction calculations each lesson.

MEASURABLE: **Refers to behaviour that can be tallied or counted.** e.g. In seat behaviour and the completion of discrete tasks.

ACHIEVABLE: **Refers to targets that the pupil has the potential to achieve .**
e.g. With effort Mary can achieve the target of increasing her time on seat by 10 minutes. (This may be based on observations of Mary attaining the target on a few past occasions. Alternatively it may be based on the fact that it is a small step that requires a minimum effort.)
The target should also relate to class norms i.e. the pupil should not be expected to achieve an absolute standard of behaviour unless of course the class as a whole has achieved it. Rather the pupil should be expected to achieve a level of behaviour that is commensurate with the class average.

RELEVANT: **Refers to targets that are related to the behavioural difficulties the pupil is experiencing.** e.g. Mary is experiencing difficulties with staying in seat and therefore needs a target that addresses that problem.

TIME-LIMITED: Refers to the target being achieved within a given time period, one that is not too long nor too short.

E. Timing and Reviews

For each intervention it is necessary to establish its probable length and course. At an appropriate time a review should take place. The length of the intervention should depend on such factors as: the nature of the problem behaviours, the severity of those behaviours, the referral point in the pupil's school career and the school's pastoral resources and organization.

ASSESSMENT TIME

An effective intervention depends on an adequate assessment of a pupil's strengths as well as weaknesses. Effective assessment should include data from many different sources:
- parents, school staff, medical records, pupil records
- records from external agencies
- interviews
- formal and informal observation. Assessment should be systematic, comprehensive and formative as well as summative. Depending on the degree of urgency assessment should take two to three weeks particularly where observation is being undertaken. This enables a reliable baseline to be established.

INTERVENTION TIME

An intervention is effective when it is appropriately matched to the pupil's behavioural/learning problem in terms of its severity and urgency. The urgency will determine how quickly the intervention begins. But considerations of urgency should not override a proper assessment of the pupil. The time an intervention takes before review depends on the severity of the problem. Review can lead to re-assessment and a new intervention. Interventions can range over weeks, months and even years. Periods of deliberate non-intervention can be used to see whether the change in behaviour will be maintained without support.

EVALUATION TIME

The evaluation can be summative, summing up the outcome of the intervention or formative leading one on to the next step.

The intervention should be evaluated by using the following criteria:
- Have the pupil target behaviours been realized e.g. in terms of frequency, intensity and duration?
- Do teachers agree on the outcome of the intervention?
- Has the intervention been running long enough to have any effect?
- Has the intervention been adequately implemented?
- The outcome of the intervention should lead to either satisfactory resolution of the problem, re-assessment leading to a new intervention or re-referral elsewhere.

F. Pupil Involvement

IN ASSESSMENT

The pupil should be asked for ways in which they would like to contribute to the assessment process. The pupil could refer for example to their reports, to particular teachers' comments, to their parents and to other pupils. This would encourage the pupil to perceive the assessment process as fair. The assessment data should be shown and discussed with the pupil.

IN THE INTERVENTION

The intervention should be discussed with the pupil in order to gain their consent and collaboration. However this consent may not be given. If the pupil is totally unco-operative then the intervention will fail from the beginning. But where there is reluctant collaboration it may be possible to proceed with the intervention if the pupil follows instructions. At least it is worth persevering to test out the situation. The intervention should be planned in a way that builds on the strengths of the pupil and it should also augment the pupil's motivation.

IN THE REVIEW

The pupil should be asked during the review period their assessment of the effects of the intervention on their behaviour/learning. Their comments might enable the teacher to gauge how far the pupil's perceptions are adrift from their own. This in turn should allow the teacher to judge what, if any, further measures are needed

G. Implementation

MONITORING OF THE PUPIL

The pupil's behaviour/learning must be monitored regularly and consistently during the intervention. This process in itself can lead to an improvement in a pupil's behaviour. It is advisable that monitoring takes the form of direct and where possible immediate, documented recording using the Pupil Assessment Profile. The PAP encourages a structured and consistent approach to monitoring.

FEEDBACK TO PUPIL / STAFF / PARENT

It is desirable that positive as well as negative feedback be provided to the pupil, staff and parents. This could be achieved through the use of the PAP as it is readily understood by pupils, staff and parents. This feedback should be presented as positively as possible in order to encourage all participants in the intervention.

REVIEW WITH PUPIL / STAFF / PARENT

Reviews should be regular and be both formative as well as summative. They should take the form ideally of all three parties looking at reports, PAPs etc. These records should be scrutinized in relation to how far the pupil has achieved their specific targets. With this in mind the following points should be considered:

- how does the current intensity, frequency and duration of the behaviour compare to the baseline?
- has there been a shift in the expectations of the parties, if so, what are the implications of this for the review?
- are there discrepancies between the perceptions of the parties involved, if so, how are these to be reconciled?
- a review may require a reassessment before a modified or new intervention is tried.
- a review also needs to consider the question of priorities as it is necessary to bear in mind that the pupil's behaviour may have improved such that other pupils become more urgent priorities.

5. Thinking About Planning

A Framework for the Process

There are many aspects of planning in the classroom. **This chapter is confined specifically to the planning aspects of helping pupils to change their view of themselves in order to move forward in the areas of learning and behaviour.**

We all at times get stuck with negative perceptions about ourselves and about the world around us. The very *idea* of achieving more can become somewhere between difficult and unimaginable. These perceptions can be an image we have formed of ourselves, our self-esteem, or can derive from external factors. The same is true of the pupils we teach. '*I'm too thick to understand this*' can be a seemingly unshakable truth, with complex roots in family and life experience. Or, such a feeling could arise from an undiagnosed partial hearing loss and the peer and staff reactions to this.

In thinking about how a pupil's negative self-perceptions interact with knowledge and skills acquisition we consider a confusing variety of factors. The purpose of the Planning Sheet suggested in this chapter is to provide a framework for this thinking. After assessment of the situation, including our own possible contribution to it, our aim is to find ways of helping the pupil to experience themselves and their abilities in a new light.

The Planning Sheet is intended for use:

- *At Stage 1 of the Code of Practice to translate the information gathered in the Profiles into practical strategies for intervention.*

- *At Stage 2/3 of the Code of Practice to form a foundation on which to approach drawing up an Individual Education Plan and plan an intervention, as discussed in the following chapter.*

The particular questions chosen for the Planning Sheet can be added to or changed for individual pupils in both cases. At Stage 1 additional questions might be based on the italicised words in the four sections on Assessment, Formulation, Intervention and Evaluation on the IEP form in Chapter 6.

When using the Planning Sheet at Stage 2 *in conjunction* with the IEP forms in Chapter 6, questions could again be added, based on the italicised words on the IEP form. When used as an aid to filling out the IEP form the Planning Sheet could be filled out using brief notes only.

When used at Stage 2/3 the Planning Sheet operates both:

- *as a tool for use with the commentary in Chapter 6 when drawing up an IEP*

- *as a framework for the process of planning running through our use of the IEP when working with a pupil over a long period of time.*

The commentary on the use of the Planning Sheet which follows is intended as a guide to this process.

Looking At Yourself and Your Classroom

Learning and behaviour happen in the context of the classroom and the school, though they might be influenced by emotional and social factors beyond this environment. As teachers, we have direct influence over the school context and can also make genuine efforts to involve parents and carers in a partnership with ourselves and others. **The more thoroughly we are prepared to examine the context over which we *do* have control, the more effective will be our partnership with pupil, parents and others. By questioning ourselves honestly and therefore being able to consider *all* ways forward, we model the possibility of change.** We are also more likely to be experienced by pupils and parents as understanding both them and the problem at hand. This understanding is equated with 'caring' and both pupil and parents are made to feel as if they *matter*.

There are a large number of questions you can usefully ask yourself about whether, and in what way, this particular pupil finds the context difficult. No classroom management style, to take one aspect of the context, is going to be the best for all pupils. In fact, though your style might be very well-suited to some pupils and satisfactory for the majority, it will probably be unsuitable for a small number.

Teaching style is an example of one aspect of the context which the pupil causing concern might find difficult. In considering whether there are changes you can make to improve the learning environment for a pupil, Hart, in *Questioning Classrooms* (a chapter in *Mongon and Hart, 1989*) suggest a list of questions which you might ask yourself as a classroom teacher. Adapted to the case of a particular pupil causing concern these are:

How is my behaviour towards this pupil.....

How is the way all the pupils behave towards each other.....

How is this pupil's perception of the school.....

How is this pupil's perception of me as a teacher.....

How is my management and organisation of the lesson.....

How are the physical conditions.....

How is this pupil's understanding of the task.....

How are my teaching methods and materials.....

How is the way language is being used.....

....affecting his or her learning / behaviour?

37

ALSO, when filling out the Planning Sheet, ask yourself the following questions:

- *Have I set aside a quiet time to ask the pupil how s/he feels about this?*

- *Have I made time to discuss the needs identified with a colleague?*

- *Are there relevant home factors? Have I consulted with parents and / or colleagues who might have this information?*

- *Where else might I find relevant information? For instance, have I looked at the School Records?*

Some of this self-questioning is quite general or gentle.

It helps if you can be a little blunt with yourself and throw in some very specific or direct questions such as:

- *Am I on time to all my lessons?*

- *Do I understand what I'm teaching and why?*

- *Do I find it interesting?*

For every expectation we hold of the pupils, there is probably a relevant question that we can ask of ourself and our own experience.

Filling In The Planning Sheet

When using the Planning Sheet we:

- *Prioritise the areas of concern.*

- *Draw together information from the assessment and observations.*

- *Weigh up possible factors which affect the pupil and think about how these interact with each other.*

- *Decide on the aim, priorities and initial strategies for action to be taken.*

- *Ensure that strategies are tried and reviewed in a calm and measured sequence over time. This helps to ensure a genuine chance of success.*

When filling out the sheet *be as specific as possible*. This will help you think clearly and is also fairer to the pupil.

Now:

- *From the Assessment Profile choose the two areas which cause you most concern. (In secondary this will also be where the pupil scores 1 or 2)*

- *Add other **areas of concern**.*

- *Fill in the Planning Sheet boxes bearing in mind the comments and suggestions starting on page 40.*

Planning Sheet

Describe the main difficulties causing concern as specifically as possible:

1)

2)

Are there other areas causing concern?

Possible contributory factors

Immediate

Background

How do staff respond?

How do other pupils respond?

What other things happen to / are avoided by the pupil?

How might these factors be reinforcing the learning difficulty / behaviour?

What strengths does the pupil have?

Have you considered the 'context issue

Describe the overall aim of any intervention to be made

What areas are to be the focus of the intervention

What is the initial strategy to be tried?

Date for initial review

Review of initial strategy

Has the duration been reduced?

Has the frequency been reduced?

Has the intensity been reduced?

What is the next strategy to be tried?

Date for review

Review of intervention

Continue on extention sheet if necessary

Possible Contributory Factors

Immediate
Think back to Chapter 3 where we outlined the ABC Chart and it's use for planning an intervention. We listed descriptions of two different kinds of Antecedents of Behaviour, immediate and background. You might find these useful in thinking about your area of concern, whether it is one of learning or behaviour. First look as specifically as possible at the situation the pupil is in and consult the headings and questions listed under Specific Antecedents, Behaviour and Consequences on the ABC Chart on page 26. Add any other questions or considerations which occur to you.

Background
Now consider the general background as it affects your concern, thinking of any factors which might have a bearing. Have you discussed the problem with the pupil's parent(s) or carers, or with a colleague who has? Consult the headings in the General Antecedents column on the ABC chart on page 26.

How do staff and parents respond?

Try and picture yourself and other staff responding to the pupil. Describe these responses as specifically and honestly as you can. You may have to link different responses to the different areas of concern you have listed. What is your picture of how the parents respond? How does their response compare to the staff response and what conflicts or anxieties might result from this for the pupil, staff or parents? How do they affect the pupil's learning or behaviour?

How do other pupils respond?

Do the same for responses of other pupils, both singly and in groups.

What other things happen to / are avoided by the pupil?

When pupils behave or fail to achieve in the ways which concern you, think carefully about and describe what happens to them. It is almost certain that the result for the pupil will also be that they, intentionally or not, avoid certain things. These might include areas of their work, contact with individual or groups of peers, conflict, etc. Could it be that the learning difficulty or behaviour which concerns you has acquired a 'life of its own'? The things that happen to or are avoided by the pupil might have become causes in their own right.

How might these factors be reinforcing the learning difficulty / behaviour?

Becoming 'causes in their own right' is another way of saying that these factors then reinforce the difficulty. This could happen in different ways. Try and think of exactly how this is happening. Is the nature of the problem changed or complicated in any way by what happens as a result of the difficulty? Or by what the pupil is avoiding, or perceives him or herself to be avoiding?

What strengths does the pupil have?

Think about the pupil afresh and look for strengths in their achievement and behaviour, whether related to your concern or not. By building on strengths and interests you might find surprising ways in to 'unlock' the difficulty the pupil is having.

Have you considered the 'context' issues? If so how might these be relevant?

The 'context' is the classroom and the school and was discussed in the section on *'Looking at Yourself and Your Classroom'* earlier in this chapter. It is always worth remembering that, from the pupil's point of view, the dominating factors in their school life are often nothing to do with our concerns of teaching and learning. Peer and playground issues, for example, might be the real structuring elements in a pupil's daily school experience, affecting behaviour and achievement, sometimes profoundly. Careful self and classroom observation put us in a stronger position to recognise and evaluate these aspects of the pupil's experience. The result may be humbling for our picture of ourselves as professionals. We need to be aware of this sense of being peripheral to pupil's experience and at the same time be aware of the apparently contradictory truth that we are also profoundly important to our pupils.

Describe the overall aim of any intervention to be made

Take some time to mull over the information from your observation and the first half of the Planning Sheet. From this try and describe your overall aim, your long term goal, with this pupil.

What areas are to be the focus of the intervention?

When you come to what areas to focus on, again give yourself a little time for thought. You might find that your aim can best be approached by concentrating on areas and short term goals which are relevant, but not immediately connected, to your overall aim, your long term goal. The point is that your overall aim *is* just that, somewhere you are trying to get to *in the end*. You might want to help the pupil to approach this point by concentrating on one or more other areas first. This can have the effect of making the journey a safer one for the pupil. Think as much as possible about the stages along the way.

What is the initial strategy to be tried?

Now break down these areas on which you've decided to focus still further, thinking of very short-term goals. Choose one of these. Think of a strategy, seeing it as a first step only, in pursuit of this goal. The point is that the strategy you choose should not be ambitious, but should make the goal achievable for the pupil. Success can then be steadily built on. The whole process will be strengthened if you can involve the pupil in setting their own goals, both long and short term, and thinking with you of strategies to achieve these.

Date for Initial Review

This is important for everyone. The period of time you choose will be a breathing space for teachers, pupil and parents alike. What is being tried is something new. People need time to adjust to new approaches and ways of doing things. The possibility for change is greater if all parties can resist the temptation to make judgements of success or failure impulsively or too soon. So offer encouragement and show you have faith in the change, and be prepared to wait and see. Put the review date in your work or Planning Diary.

Review of Initial Strategy

When reviewing the initial strategy remember to do this only in terms of the limited, short-term goals which were set. Discuss with other colleagues (and parents if possible) to find out what their impression of how things have gone is before giving yours. What does the pupil think? Think about the way in which the strategy has succeeded or failed and what can be learned from this. Think about the balance between success and failure, rather than trying to decide neatly which was achieved. Were the goals immediate, limited and achievable? Could they have been safely extended a little?

If the strategy was about behaviour think about whether the duration, frequency and intensity of the behaviour has altered. If the strategy was to help in an area of the pupil's learning think about how these measures might be helpful to you and to the pupil in thinking about progress and change. Talking about problems which seem intractable and hopeless to the pupil in factual terms like these might help them to acknowledge and accept progress. A small enhancement of self-esteem can be a building block for the success of your next strategy.

What is the next strategy to be tried?

It might be useful now to refer back to your overall aim and to think about what other areas you want to cover and stages you might have to go through. Think of all the aspects of your review of the first strategy in relation to this. Do you want to concentrate on exactly the same area, possibly to extend the goals slightly, keeping them achievable? Or might it be more productive to shift the emphasis slightly? How does the pupil feel about it? How can you help the pupil to believe realistically in the possibility of change and how can you adapt the strategy you choose to this end?

Again, describe the strategy you work out clearly and tie it to a goal that is limited, specific and achievable. Be clear how it relates to your overall aim. If the pupil is involved in the process you might have to help them to keep things modest, to see it as an opportunity to succeed, not a challenge to make them anxious.

Date for Review

In light of the experience of the first review, do you need to extend or shorten the period to give the strategy a fair chance? How does this timescale fit into the timescale you have in mind for your overall aim? Again, it is important to stick to the time you have allowed, however tempting it might be to say *'It's hopeless'* or *'It's obviously working, let's make it harder'*.

Review of intervention

The Planning Sheet is intended as the basis of a way of working. This Review is therefore not to be seen as a final evaluation, but as part of an on-going evaluation process. Bear in mind some of the points made in the section on *'Review of Initial Strategy'*. Also look at the section on Evaluation in Chapter 6. There the importance of measuring change against both a baseline of where the pupil started from in specific terms and against others in the class is discussed.

Come to the Review with an open mind and an eye on specific changes in learning and behaviour over the period, rather than an impression of how things have been over the last day or two. Compare accurate descriptions, not random anecdotes. Listen carefully to others, as it will help you to step back from the day-to-day 'stuck' feelings we all succumb to. Be prepared to be surprised.

You might find that there are other stages which it would be productive to help the pupil negotiate. How does the pupil feel about the quality of attention she or he is receiving? Is it perceived as pressure or welcomed? You might want to build in some gaps where nothing is being tried and the pupil can 'coast'. This could be articulated to the pupil, helping them to feel understood. Or the pupil might be responding very well to this approach and could become more involved in setting goals and thinking of strategies. Or might just need the structure and containment implicit in this way of working?

You might want to re-think your overall aim in light of what you've learned, maybe finding that you now have greater sensitivity to the pupil's needs.

The process is on-going. It can become a productive way of working.

6. Developing IEPs

These notes are intended as a guide to drawing up IEPs at Stages 2 and 3 of the Code of Practice. It should be remembered that formats may vary from LEA to LEA or even between schools. These note focus on EBD and Literacy IEPs.

General points about IEPs:

IEPs should meet the following requirements:

Assess the pupil's difficulties

Outline an intervention

State the SEN provision required

Include staff, parents or carers involved in supporting the pupil

Discuss the IEP and its implementation with the pupil

Specify the intervention(s) and any materials needed

Set SMART targets

Establish success criteria for evaluating the intervention

Determine time scale required and state review date and arrangements

The examples of Behaviour IEPs included in this book are intended as suggestions rather than definitive exemplars. They are meant to be guides to ways in which Behaviour IEPs **could be** written in terms of format and content.

These IEPs are structured according to the following model:

Identification of pupil giving Cause for Concern with regard to behaviour and literacy

Assessment of Pupil's Difficulties

Formulation of Pupil's Difficulties

Intervention used with Pupil

Evaluation of Intervention(s)

It should be noted that there are different types of assessments and interventions which can be used singly or in combination. The choice of assessment and intervention will depend on how one:

Identifies the difficulty i.e. the criteria used to select the pupil as a cause for concern

Thinks it is caused and why it persists

Thinks it is best addressed

Differences and disagreements may occur between those people involved in the process of contributing to an IEP. These differences will reflect the points raised above. It may be necessary to reach a working consensus where disagreement occurs but it is wise to avoid unwarranted speculation and high level inferences. The reason for this is that assertions can be made about pupils based purely on anecdote or without adequate evidence being presented.

Identification of the Pupil:

The pupil will already be identified as having a difficulties by class / subject teachers, form tutor, Head of Year, Head of Department, parent or carer. Information will be collected and collated by the class teacher or form tutor and the SENCO consulted. This is STAGE 1 of the Code of Practice. A response may be made at this stage to rectify the pupil's difficulties and meet the pupil's needs. The pupil will have been placed on the SEN register.

At STAGE 2 of the Code of Practice, if concern continues, further assessment may be necessary. An IEP should be drawn up with the SENCO undertaking

---

Individual Education Plan (E.B.D.) | **SEN Stage 2/3**

PUPIL DETAILS | Name [ ] | DoB [ ]
Form / Class [ ] | Attendance (%): [ ] | M / F
Home Language [ ] | Ethnicity [ ]

ASSESSMENT — Underline relevent *italicised* words

ASSESSMENT INSTRUMENTS eg: Observation – formal / informal Checklist Rating Scale. Self-monitoring form School reports / forms / medicals Questionnaires Interviews
ASSESSORS eg: Parents / Carers Teachers / other staff Pupils External agencies
CONTEXTS eg: Classroom Playground Corridors Gym Assembly Toilets Office

ASSESSMENT SUMMARY: Specific description of main difficulties

FORMULATION — Underline relevent *italicised* words

FORMULATION: eg Functional analysis using ABC model
State reasons WHY the difficulties occur taking into consideration eg:
Home background Teaching styles Teaching materials / methods Learning styles
Learning difficulties Classroom management techniques Whole school factors
'Within - pupil factors' Medical reasons Attributions Lack of appropriate social skills

---

INTERVENTION

State SPECIFIC TARGETS in POSITIVE TERMS
1) ....
2) ....
3) ....
4) ....

State INTERVENTION STRATEGIES Underline relevent *italicised* words
Positive reinforcement programme Monitoring charts Report cards Contracts
Self-management programme Individual / client-centred / behavioural / group counselling
Circle work Time out Token economy Social skills training Assertiveness training
Peer-tutoring Classroom management skills Curricular differentiation
Literacy / Numeracy / Language programme etc
Other:

NAME those involved with the INTERVENTION (use initials)
Parents / Carers Teachers / Other staff Other pupils Governors External agencies etc

AGREE the duration of the INTERVENTION eg: Days / Weeks / Terms(s)
Establish START DATE: Establish REVIEW DATE:

EVALUATION Underline relevent *italicised* words

COMPARE the behaviour of the pupil BEFORE and AFTER the intervention
Use ASSESSMENT METHODS that were employed originally and include assessments
undertaken by: parents / carers teachers / other staff pupils external agencies.
SUMMARIZE review:

---

the lead rôle in assessing the pupil, planning an intervention, monitoring its implementation and reviewing its effectiveness.

Estimations of the prevalence of pupils with difficulties vary according to definitions and criteria. This being the case, whether a given pupil is perceived as having problems may simply reflect a teacher's idiosyncratic judgment. Other pupils may have the same difficulties but for some reason are not be perceived as a cause for concern. Thus it is necessary to ensure that information is collected from all staff teaching the pupil and also from parents / carers and other relevant sources. Ideally such pupils should be discussed at a highlighting or referral meeting where an informed decision can be made particularly with regard to a school's priorities.

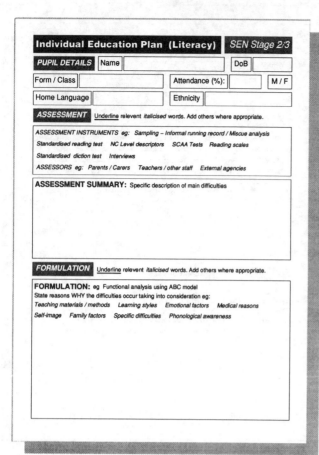

Individual Education Plan (Literacy) — SEN Stage 2/3

PUPIL DETAILS — Name _____ DoB _____

Form / Class _____ Attendance (%): _____ M / F

Home Language _____ Ethnicity _____

ASSESSMENT <u>Underline</u> relevent *italicised* words. Add others where appropriate.

ASSESSMENT INSTRUMENTS eg: Sampling – Informal running record / Miscue analysis
Standardised reading test   NC Level descriptors   SCAA Tests   Reading scales
Standardised diction test   Interviews
ASSESSORS eg: Parents / Carers   Teachers / other staff   External agencies

ASSESSMENT SUMMARY: Specific description of main difficulties

FORMULATION <u>Underline</u> relevent *italicised* words. Add others where appropriate.

FORMULATION: eg Functional analysis using ABC model
State reasons WHY the difficulties occur taking into consideration eg:
Teaching materials / methods   Learning styles   Emotional factors   Medical reasons
Self-image   Family factors   Specific difficulties   Phonological awareness

Assessment of the Pupil:

Assessment may be undertaken by teachers, parents and the pupils themselves. This may result in a lack of consensus. Where this happens it is wise for teachers and parents and if possible the pupil to find areas where a compromise is possible and desirable. The aim of assessment should be to describe the pupil's difficulties as precisely and specifically as possible. The assessment should draw on information from a variety of sources. Participants should be aware of the problems that may result from a high level of inference e.g. unsubstantiated generalizations about the pupil's behaviour. Bias may contaminate an assessment through a teacher exaggerating a pupil's negative behaviours and failing to notice the same pupil's positive behaviours or failing to notice that other pupils display the same behaviours. This may be due to the teacher's preconceptions or even dislike of the pupil. Bias may also be reflected in the way a teacher interacts with the pupil.

Teachers should state who has contributed to the assessment and the methods they have used. The IEP form itself can act as a prompt for teachers in terms of the ways in which their pupils can be assessed.

Formulation:

A formulation is based on an assessment and consists of a statement as to why the literacy or behaviour difficulty has occurred and why it continues to exist. This statement takes the form of a hypothesis. The hypothesis under

INTERVENTION <u>Underline</u> relevent *italicised* words. Add others where appropriate.

State SPECIFIC TARGETS in POSITIVE TERMS
1) ....
2) ....
3) ....
4) ....

Indicate INTERVENTION STRATEGIES
Structured reading programme   Extended choice of material   Curricular differentiation
Home-school literacy initiative   Word bank / word book programme   Spelling proagramme
Peer-tutoring   Paired reading programme   Precision teaching programme   DISTAR
Reading recovery programme

NAME those involved with the INTERVENTION (use initials)
Parents / Carers   Class / form teacher   SENCO   English / LAP teacher
Other pupils   External agencies etc

AGREE the duration of the INTERVENTION eg: Days / Weeks / Terms(s)
Establish START DATE: Establish REVIEW DATE:

EVALUATION

COMPARE the behaviour of the pupil BEFORE and AFTER the intervention
Use ASSESSMENT METHODS that were employed originally and include assessments
undertaken by: Parents / Carers   Teachers / other staff   Pupils   External agencies.
SUMMARIZE review:

consideration will be tested through an intervention. If the intervention is successful then the hypothesis will be seen as confirmed. If the intervention is unsuccessful then the hypothesis is found wanting and reformulation is required.

For behaviour difficulties, the attribution of causes or reasons can be both problematic and controversial, for example:

Unfounded speculation can occur through uncritically accepting anecdote and rumour

Allowing prejudice or dislike to cloud one's judgment

Imposing a favoured psychological perspective or framework that does not apply to the particular pupil e.g. stating that a pupil's misbehaviour must result from unconscious emotional conflicts (psychodynamic) when it is due to the learning of inappropriate behaviour (behaviourist) or vice versa

A child-deficit model may be rigidly adhered to possibly disguising the interactive nature of behavioural difficulties.

A pupil's behaviour may be the result of negative interactions between particular teachers and the pupil concerned. If this is the case, the pupil's behavioural problems should not be seen as simply a result of deficiencies or deficits in the pupil but that the teacher contributes to the problem as well. Similarly other factors may contribute to the pupil's problems e.g. the curriculum, streaming and parental attitudes. It may not be possible for teachers to influence or change these factors. Unsubstantiated generalization from a small number of incidents or from a few lessons e.g. a pupil is unfairly described as a severe behaviour problem on the basis of limited evidence. The formulation should lead to an appropriate intervention.

Intervention:

Teachers should decide on what kind or kinds of intervention are likely to address the pupil's difficulties. These interventions should be agreed by all the participants concerned and be carried out collaboratively. The intervention should be implemented within a specified time frame along with a date for review, interventions should be carefully selected with regard to:

The pupil's specific problems

Availability of staff, time and resources

Availability of specialist expertise among the staff

The degree of commitment of staff, parents and pupils

Interventions should be implemented in terms of a limited number of specific positive targets. It is unrealistic to expect pupils to fulfil a large number of targets particularly if they are vague. In other words the targets should be SMART. Interventions should be given a reasonable time to succeed and relevant success criteria should have been drawn up prior to the intervention so that all participants are aware of what is required.

Evaluation:

Teachers should evaluate the success or otherwise of the intervention(s). This can be achieved through comparing the pupil's behaviour with the pre-intervention baseline. this should enable teachers to ascertain whether there has been an improvement or deterioration in the pupil's difficulties. Alternatively, the pupil's difficulties may not have changed at all. For behaviour difficulties, teachers should also consider the pupil's behaviour in relation to other pupils in the class and to the behaviour of the class as a whole.

Failure to use a pre-intervention baseline makes it difficult to detect improvements in a pupil's behaviour. Teachers may arrive at impressionistic judgments as to how much or little the pupil has changed.

Failure to compare the pupil's behaviour to other pupils or to the class's behaviour may lead to unrealistic expectations of what the referred pupil is able to achieve.

Failure of an intervention may be attributable to a single factor or a combination of factors, for instance:

> *Targets being too vague or too many participants*
>
> *Teachers, parents and pupil being uncommitted to the intervention*
>
> *Being poorly implemented or not implemented at all*
>
> *Success criteria not being agreed*
>
> *Type of intervention inappropriate for the pupil's difficulties*

Individual Education Plan (Literacy) — SEN Stage 2/3

PUPIL DETAILS

| Name | Mary Williams | DoB | 13.12.85 |

| Form / Class | HB. | Attendance (%): | 90% | M / F |

| Home Language | | Ethnicity | |

ASSESSMENT — Underline relevent *italicised* words. Add others where appropriate.

ASSESSMENT INSTRUMENTS eg: *Sampling – Informal running record / Miscue analysis*

Standardised reading test   *NC Level descriptors*   *SATs*   *Reading scales*

Standardised diction test   *Interviews*

ASSESSORS eg: *Parents / Carers,* *Teachers / other staff*   *External agencies*

ASSESSMENT SUMMARY: Specific description of main difficulties

IEPs: Problems That May Arise

At times certain problems may arise when it comes to planning and implementing behaviour IEPs. It is wise to consider those problems before drawing up an IEP. In some instances, problems related to behaviour may also apply to literacy difficulties.

General:

Inadequate experience and training: Staff may lack adequate experience or training in working collaboratively in developing and implementing IEPs.

Insufficient staff, time and resources: IEPs may be drawn up without recognition of the fact that there might be insufficient resources, personnel or time to plan or implement them.

Unrealistic planning: IEPs may be unrealistic and not relate to the conditions actually existing in the school and classrooms.

Parents / carers lack of confidence: Parents or carers may lack the necessary confidence to contribute to the IEP process.

Specific:

Lack of consensus regarding the pupil's behaviour difficulties: Parents may state that they have no problems with their child at home and as a result find it difficult to understand or believe that their child has significant problems at school. Teachers may perceive the pupil differently some experiencing behaviour difficulties with the pupil other teachers having no problems. Where there is agreement that the pupil has problems, there still may be differences over the appropriate target behaviours the pupil should achieve.

Disagreement over the reasons or causes of the pupil's behaviour difficulties: Where there is agreement on the nature of a pupil's behaviour difficulties there still may be differences of opinion on what creates and maintains those problems. Parents may see teachers as responsible for their child's behaviour by the way they deal with their child. Some teachers in turn may attribute the child's problem to the parents who they see as exercising inadequate or inconsistent discipline. Other teachers may hold a child- deficit model and attribute the pupil's difficulties to the child's temperament.

Disagreement over strategies for dealing with a pupil's misbehaviour: Teachers and parents may disagree over behaviour strategies. Some teachers may think that the main responsibility lies with the parents and that they should discipline their child more effectively. Other teachers may think the pupil needs psychotherapy. In turn parents may see the teachers as lacking appropriate behaviour management skills for dealing with their child and suggest that teachers acquire those skills.

Pupil refusal or reluctance to co-operate with an IEP: The pupil may be antagonistic towards having an IEP. It may be seen as stigmatizing or as being too demanding.

Disagreement over evaluation of the intervention: Teachers may disagree over whether a target behaviour has been achieved. This may arise because teachers are using different success criteria or have conflicting expectations of the pupil.

Primary Case Study

The case studies are not offered as definitive in any way. They show one way in which IEPs could be written. Schools may wish to base their IEPs on these examples or they may provide ideas on how schools might construct their own. Schools may even see them as totally impracticable!

The IEP forms themselves are intended to allow easy and rapid recording of information as well as being informative with regard to assessment, formulation and intervention. Assessment methods, formulation factors and interventions are just suggestions. Each school will need to decide for itself what is practicable and desirable. Schools would also have to decide how much detail (for example as shown in the case studies) they would write down on the IEP forms.

Identification:

John is a NC Year 6 boy in a Junior School and is aged 10yrs 6mths. John was identified by his class teacher as a cause for concern with respect to his behavioural difficulties in the classroom. John has behavioural problems that interfere with his own learning and that of other pupils' in his class.

Assessment – Methods:

John was assessed through formal and informal observation and his class teacher completed assessment forms on him. He was interviewed using a structured interview form. His parents had been contacted and agreed to the assessment process. They also provided information on John from their own experience. and completed a questionnaire. A functional analysis of his behaviour was undertaken using the ABC. The teacher also completed a Primary Assessment Profile (PAP) form. A Fixed Interval Sampling Sheet and a Behaviour Frequency Sheet were used for formal observation.

Assessment – Profile:

The accumulated information provides the basis for the following assessment:

> John in the classroom is frequently off task - shouting out to the teacher and other pupils, leaving his seat frequently and then interfering with or distracting other pupils. He also pull faces and make jokes. Other pupils are distracted by him at first, laughing at his antics but then return to their work, ignoring him. He finds it difficult to read and is significantly below the class norm.

> At home John's parents see him as lacking in ability and as very trying as he is constantly disobedient. He is the youngest of three children and is seen by his parents as not as bright as the other two, who are both secondary aged girls.

> Using the ABC it is apparent that John's classroom behaviour is a particular problem when he is asked to read (an antecedent). Through his behaviour John gains the attention of the teacher and other pupils, this attention and the

avoidance of reading (consequences) reinforces this behaviour.

At home John is unfavourably compared with his "brighter" sisters and he reacts by being disobedient.

A baseline has been established drawing on information from observation and assessment forms:- He is out of his seat 60% of the time during a period of 1 hour and on task for 30% of the same period of time. He shouts out approximately 6 times every hour to the teacher and / or pupils.

Formulation:

John has low self-esteem linked to his reading difficulties. He engages in attention seeking behaviour which reinforces his behaviour and which enables him to feel noticed. He is gaining attention in inappropriate ways by disturbing the class.

Intervention:

Aims:

1. To enable John to improve his self-esteem through:
   Expanding his reading skills.

   Gaining appropriate attention and reinforcement from his class teacher, parents and other pupils.

2. To increase John's on-seat time.

3. To enable John to make his requests for appropriate attention quietly and politely.

Interventions – For Classroom / For Home:

Behaviour monitoring book:

John is to help the teacher to design a behaviour book using the computer. The book will be taken home by John and he will also have a similar book at home with three targets relevant to behaviour at home. Behaviour monitoring book with three SMART targets for John to achieve for instance:

> *1. Asking quietly for the teacher's attention.*

> *2. Politely asking other pupils to help him with his work.*

> *3. Staying in seat.*

Rewards will be provided by the class teacher on successful achievement of target behaviours e.g. allow John to use the computer more or engage in any other preferred activity for a longer period of time. If John behaves particularly well over an extended period he will be able to go on a trip he chooses.

Class teacher:

The teacher will try to ignore John's minor disruptive behaviour and praise him for positive behaviour. If John persists in misbehaving he will sent out of the room for a limited period of time (time-out). The teacher will arrange for John to have more help with his reading by increasing time with him and in a reading withdrawal group. Peer-tutoring: Other pupils will be asked if they would like to help John with his reading and form a support group to help him in his efforts to improve his behaviour.

Parents:

The parents have agreed to help John with his reading. The parents have also agreed to monitor his behaviour book and reward John for successfully achieving his school targets. They have also decided to set him target behaviours for home and have linked rewards to them. If John is particularly badly behaved they will withdraw privileges or impose sanctions.

Evaluation:

A review date has been agreed with the parents. The interventions will be evaluated using observation, questionnaires and interviews. The class teacher, parents and the pupil will be able to present their views on progress towards the target behaviours.

Conclusion of:

The class teacher and parents agree that his reading has improved and that as a result his self-esteem has increased.

He is now out of his seat less than 10% during a 1 hour period and on task for 70% of the same period of time.

His parents state that he has gone a long way in achieving their targets at home.

John says he thinks he is doing better with his reading and that he stays in his seat longer and does not shout out or interrupt as much as he did before.

Individual Education Plan   (E.B.D.)   *SEN Stage 2/3*

PUPIL DETAILS	Name		DoB	
Form / Class		Attendance (%):		M / F
Home Language		Ethnicity		

ASSESSMENT   Underline relevent *italicised* words. Add others where appropriate.

ASSESSMENT INSTRUMENTS eg: Observation – formal / informal   Checklist   Rating Scale.

Self-monitoring form   School reports / forms / medicals   Questionnaires   Interviews

ASSESSORS eg: Parents / Carers   Teachers / other staff   Pupils   External agencies

CONTEXTS eg: Classroom   Playground   Corridors   Gym   Assembly   Toilets   Office

ASSESSMENT SUMMARY: Specific description of main difficulties

Secondary Case Study

Identification:

Mary is a NC Year 9 girl in a Mixed Secondary Comprehensive and is aged 13 yrs 7mths. Mary is identified by her form tutor, her HOY and six of her subject teachers as a major cause for concern - in English, French, Maths, History, Geography and RE. Mary is identified by other subject teachers as a minor cause for concern in - Drama, PE, Art, Music, Technology and IT. Mary is seen as having behavioural problems that interfere with her learning and that of other pupils'.

Assessment – methods:

Mary has been observed formally using a Fixed Interval Sampling sheet and also informally. She has been interviewed using a structured questionnaire form. Information from her subject teachers has been collected using Secondary Assessment Profile (SAP) forms and collated on the SAP Grid. Functional analyses of Mary's behaviour were undertaken by her subject teachers using the ABC. Mary's mother has also been interviewed using a structured questionnaire form.

Mary's classroom behaviour is a particular problem when she is asked to write (an antecedent). She tends to shout out to the boys who respond similarly. The consequences are that she avoids writing and encourages the boys to retaliate. Her unwillingness to write is not related to any deficit in terms of reading or writing skills.

Assessment – profile:

The accumulated information provides the basis for the following assessment:

Mary is frequently off task in the classroom - shouting out to teachers and pupils - this behaviour being much less frequent in practical subjects. Mary engages in constant off task talking with other girls in the class and abusive exchanges with some of the boys.

Mary also gets involved in confrontations with teachers as a result of her interrupting lessons.

Mary lacks confidence when it comes to writing although her reading is adequate in terms of understanding the material presented in lessons. She prefers practical subjects as she does not have to do so much writing and she has as one of her strengths a talent for drawing and painting.

At home Mary's mother (one-parent family) finds her disobedient and moody. Mary will answer back and sulk if not given her own way. There is an older brother in the family who has recently left school and who is also living at home. She constantly has arguments with him.

Using the ABC, it is apparent that if teachers ask Mary to write (an antecedent) she starts shouting out to teachers and to boys in the lessons and the (consequences) are that the boys retaliate and the teacher reprimands or sends Mary out of the room.

INTERVENTION

State SPECIFIC TARGETS in POSITIVE TERMS

1)

2)

3)

4)

Underline relevent *italicised* words

*Positive reinforcement programme   Monitoring charts   Report cards   Contracts
Self-management programme   Individual / client-centred / behavioural / group counselling
Circle work   Time out   Token economy   Social skills training   Assertiveness training
Peer-tutoring   Classroom management skills   Curricular differentiation
Literacy / Numeracy / Language programme etc
Other:*

NAME those involved with the INTERVENTION (use initials)
Parents / Carers   Teachers / Other staff   Other pupils   Governors   External agencies etc

AGREE the duration of the INTERVENTION eg: *Days / Weeks / Terms(s)*
Establish START DATE: Establish REVIEW DATE:

EVALUATION   Underline relevent *italicised* words

COMPARE the behaviour of the pupil BEFORE and AFTER the intervention
Use ASSESSMENT METHODS that were employed originally and include assessments
undertaken by: *parents / carers   teachers / other staff   pupils   external agencies.*
SUMMARIZE review:

Designed by Francesca Gray and Harry Ayers

A rough baseline has been established using informal observation and information drawn from the SAPs which indicate that in subjects where she has to write frequently she shouts out on average 6 times an hour but in practical lessons about twice an hour. She is also off-task on average 50% of the time in lessons which require more writing and 10% in those that do not.

Formulation:

Mary displays frequent off-task behaviours (shouting out and refusing to write) in those lessons where she is asked by teachers to produce a lot of written work. In practical subjects her off-task behaviour is relatively infrequent. Her behaviour is the result of her reluctance to write and the attention she gains from other pupils. By shouting out she avoids writing and gains attention, these consequences reinforcing the negative behaviour.

Intervention:

Aims / Positive targets:

1. To enable Mary to improve her self-confidence through:
   Increasing her writing output. so that she feels more confident in this area.
   Gaining appropriate attention and reinforcement from her subject teachers   and class peers so that she does not experience negative comments from teachers and abusive remarks from other pupils.

2. To raise Mary's level of achievement in all subject areas through:
   Encouraging Mary to increase her output of written work and to improve the quality of her work

Specific Interventions – For Classroom / For Home

Writing reinforcement programme:
Voucher - points system: Mary will receive a point for each piece of completed writing and 10 points will equal I merit and 10 merits will earn her a £10 voucher which can be used to purchase a cassette or a book. The HOY and Form Tutor will supervise and monitor the programme. This programme will be used at home by Mary's mother to reward Mary for compliance with her mother's requests.

Behaviour management techniques:
This programme will be used at home by Mary's mother to reward Mary for compliance with her mother's requests.

Initially at the beginning of her lessons subject teachers will help Mary start a piece of writing by providing five minutes of support. During lesson time teachers will offer Mary additional but brief support with her writing.

Subject teachers will ask Mary to raise her hand when requesting help.They will try and ignore her if she shouts out for help and praise her if she raises her hand.

Mary will be on a tailor-made weekly monitoring card which will state positive and specific targets. This card will be checked by Mary's mother as well as by the school.

Grouping / seating arrangements:

Mary will be seated on her own to begin with but if she completes the written work set she will be allowed for a trial period to sit with her friend conditional on her being polite to the teacher and other pupils. She must continue to complete the work set if she is to remain sitting with her friend.

Cognitive-behavioural counselling:

The year head sees Mary at the end of the week to check her monitoring book and to discuss problems, problem-solving strategies and possible consequences with Mary. Where Mary has made progress the year head praises Mary and where there have been problems the year head discusses with Mary ways of resolving those problems. If those problems are continuing the year head outlines the possible consequences of unresolved problems.

Evaluation:

Mary's progress towards the agreed targets will be based on post-intervention observation, structured interview questionnaires, SAPs and functional analysis after a period of seven weeks has elapsed.

The school and Mary's mother will need to agree on success criteria in terms of what constitutes sufficient progress towards the targets.

After seven weeks Mary has increased her written work by roughly 50% and teachers have been able to praise her frequently for her on-task behaviour. Teachers have also been able to praise her fairly frequently for requesting support in a polite manner. She has more positive exchanges with other pupils. At home Mary is more polite to her mother and even asks on occasion if she wants help with household chores. Mary avoids arguing with her brother.

If this level of improvement is deemed sufficient the school may decide to simply monitor Mary's behaviour over the next 7 weeks. If there has been some but not sufficient progress then the same interventions may continue for another seven weeks. If there is no or very little progress then there may be a need for a reassessment.

Subject teachers will try to ignore Mary's shouting out where possible and praise her when she completes a piece of work and where she speaks quietly. Grouping / seating arrangements: Mary will be allowed to sit with her friends conditional on her not shouting out and producing satisfactory work.

Photocopiable Sheets

Primary Assessment Profile (sides 1 – 2)

Secondary Assessment Profile (sides 1 – 2)

Secondary Score Sheet

Class Monitoring Sheet

Planning Sheet (sides 1 – 2)

Fixed Interval Sampling Sheet

Frequency Count Sheet

ABC of Behaviour Sheet

Pupil Observation Sheet

Pupil Interview Sheet (sides 1 – 3)

Parent / Carer Interview Sheet (sides 1 – 3)

Behaviour IEP (sides 1 – 2)

Literacy IEP (sides 1 – 2)

Primary Assessment Profile *(Original version)*

Secondary Assessment Profile *(Original version)*

Secondary Score Sheet *(Original version)*

Primary Assessment Profile

Pupil [ ] N C Year [ ] Date [ ][ ][ ]

Class [ ] E2L Stage: *1 2 3 4* Home Language [ ]

Gender: *M / F* Medical [ ] Teacher [ ]

On each continuum, circle the appropriate number. When indicating behaviour consider only the last 6 weeks. Underline example words which you think are appropriate, adding others which you think describe the pupil's difficulties or achievements

Average or Acceptable

Concern → 1 2 3 4 5 *← Excellent*

---

1) Attendance [ ] % age   *1 2 3 4 5*

2) Punctuality   *1 2 3 4 5*

LEARNING / WORK
English
1) Speaking and Listening Level [ ]

2) Reading Level [ ]

3) Writing Level [ ]

Mathematics

1) Using and Applying Maths Level [ ]

2) Number and Algebra Level [ ]

3) Shape, Space and Measuring Level [ ]

4) Handling Data Level [ ]

Science

1) Experimental and Investigative Science Level [ ]

2) Life processes and Living Things Level [ ]

3) Materials and Properties Level [ ]

4) Physical Processes Level [ ]

Do these results reflect the pupil's potential?

Comments on other subject areas:
(Indicate levels of subjects which are below or above average)

---

3) Starting work   *1 2 3 4 5*

Needs to have things very clearly explained
Frequently finds an excuse / Has to be prompted to start
Wants to do something different

4) Working cooperatively   *1 2 3 4 5*

Chats a lot / Dominates / Fails to work with others
Finds it difficult to share

5) Work   *1 2 3 4 5*

Work usually unfinished / Badly presented
Only finishes work if kept in / Lack of care or pride
Destroys own work / Easily becomes discouraged
Copies other people / Seems satisfied with very little

6) Organisational skills   *1 2 3 4 5*

Loses work / Fails to bring equipment

7) Working independently   *1 2 3 4 5*

Always asking for help   *Gets on well by themselves*
Fails to work on own

8) Managing difficulties in work   *1 2 3 4 5*

Quickly gets frustrated / Gives up / Avoids work
Needs a lot of reassurance and help
Finds it difficult to remember things
Finds it difficult to concentrate

From **Assessing Individual Needs** – H. Ayers, D. Clarke and A. Ross – *David Fulton Publishers – 1996*

PERSONAL and SOCIAL

9) Self-confidence   *1 2 3 4 5*
Copes with difficulties, appears worried   *Recognises own successes*
Over-reacts to events   *Can be given responsibilities*
Demands attention

10) Awareness of other's needs *1 2 3 4 5*
Seems only concerned about themselves   *Can listen to others*
Inappropriate helpfulness   *Helpful to staff, helpful to peers*
Shows insight into others' situations

11) Self-awareness   *1 2 3 4 5*
Can discuss difficulties   *Can express feelings appropriately*
Reacts defensively / denies having difficulties
Doesn't seem to take responsibility for own actions

12) Following instructions   *1 2 3 4 5*
Unable to follow simple instructions
Able to follow complicated instructions
Frequently needs reassurance

13) Friendship   *1 2 3 4 5*
Has no friends   *Has friends*
Fails to make positive contact
Tends to follow, Dominates others

14) Responding to correction *1 2 3 4 5*
Over-reacts   *Responds well and changes behaviour*
Accepts correction with difficulty

15) Managing disagreements   *1 2 3 4 5*
Gets into lots of disagreements
Disagreements often end in a fight

16) Managing in the playground *1 2 3 4 5*
Finds it difficult to join in   *Plays well with others*
Gets picked on

BEHAVIOUR

17) Interactions with peers   *1 2 3 4 5*
Physically aggressive, verbally aggressive
Works well with others, Finds it difficult to join in
Gets picked on, Teased

18) Interactions with adults   *1 2 3 4 5*
Physically aggressive, verbally aggressive
Withdrawn, Provoking, Attention demanding

19) Use of equipment   *1 2 3 4 5*
Misuse of equipment, furniture or materials
Minor vandalism, Major vandalism

20) Pupil noise   *1 2 3 4 5*
Constant talking to peers, Shouting out
Interrupting teacher, Non-verbal noises
Tapping

21) Movement about the class *1 2 3 4 5*
Wandering about, moving around on the mat
Interfering with others, Leaving the room

22) Public areas   *1 2 3 4 5*
Corridors, Playground, Assembly, Toilets, Office
Physical / Verbal aggression to staff / pupils
Intentional / unintentional interference of others
Noise, Misuse of equipment, Graffiti, Litter

23) How does the pupil's behaviour compare with others in the class?

Much worse	Worse	Average	Better	Much Better
1	*2*	*3*	*4*	*5*

Please indicate any areas of strength or improvements made recently:

Please indicate two areas that you are concerned about:

Please indicate any strategies you have found useful:

From **Assessing Individual Needs** – H. Ayers, D. Clarke and A. Ross – *David Fulton Publishers – 1996*

Secondary Assessment Profile

Pupil _____ Form ____ N C Year ____ Date ____

Form Tutor _____ Gender: **M / F** Subject _____

Home Language _____ E2L Stage: **1 2 3 4** Medical _____

On each continuum, circle the appropriate number. When indicating behaviour consider only the last 6 weeks. <u>Underline example words which you think are appropriate,</u> adding others which you think describe the pupil's difficulties or achievements

Average or Acceptable
↓
Concern → 1 2 3 4 5 ← Excellent

1) Attendance ☐ % age 1 2 3 4 5   **2) Punctuality** 1 2 3 4 5

LEARNING / WORK

Fill in Attainment Targets as appropriate

AT 1 Level or KS ☐   **AT 2** Level or KS ☐

AT 3 Level or KS ☐   **AT 4** Level or KS ☐

General comments about subject:

Do these results reflect the pupil's potential?

3) Standard of work 1 2 3 4 5

4) Starting work 1 2 3 4 5
Needs to have things very clearly explained
Frequently finds an excuse / Has to be prompted to start
Wants to do something different

5) Work 1 2 3 4 5
Work usually unfinished / badly presented
Only finishes work if kept in / Lack of care or pride
Destroys own work / Easily becomes discouraged
Copies other people / Seems satisfied with very little

6) Working cooperatively 1 2 3 4 5
Chats a lot / Dominates   Fails to work with others
Finds it difficult to share

7) Working independently 1 2 3 4 5
Always asking for help   Gets on well by themselves
Fails to work on own

8) Organisational skills 1 2 3 4 5
Loses work / Fails to bring equipment

9) Managing difficulties in work 1 2 3 4 5
Quickly gets frustrated, Gives up, Avoids work
Needs a lot of reassurance and help
Finds it difficult to remember things
Finds it difficult to concentrate

From **Assessing Individual Needs** – H. Ayers, D. Clarke and A. Ross – *David Fulton Publishers – 1996*

PERSONAL and SOCIAL

10) Self-confidence *1 2 3 4 5*
Copes with difficulties, appears worried *Recognises own successes*
Over-reacts to events *Can be given responsibilities*
Demands attention

11) Awareness of other's needs *1 2 3 4 5*
Seems only concerned about themselves *Can listen to others*
Inappropriate helpfulness *Helpful to staff, helpful to peers*
Shows insight into others' situations

12) Self-awareness *1 2 3 4 5*
Can discuss difficulties *Can express feelings appropriately*
Reacts defensively / denies having difficulties
Doesn't seem to take responsibility for own actions

13) Following instructions *1 2 3 4 5*
Unable to follow simple instructions
Able to follow complicated instructions
Frequently needs reassurance

14) Friendship *1 2 3 4 5*
Has no friends *Has friends*
Fails to make positive contact
Tends to follow, Dominates others

15) Responding to correction *1 2 3 4 5*
Over-reacts *Responds well and changes behaviour*
Accepts correction with difficulty

16) Managing disagreements *1 2 3 4 5*
Gets into lots of disagreements
Disagreements often end in a fight

17) Managing in the playground *1 2 3 4 5*
Finds it difficult to join in *Plays well with others*
Gets picked on

BEHAVIOUR

18) Interactions with peers *1 2 3 4 5*
Physically aggressive, verbally aggressive
Works well with others, Finds it difficult to join in
Gets picked on, Teased

19) Interactions with adults *1 2 3 4 5*
Physically aggressive, verbally aggressive
Withdrawn, Provoking, Attention demanding

20) Use of equipment *1 2 3 4 5*
Misuse of equipment, furniture or materials
Minor vandalism, Major vandalism

21) Pupil noise *1 2 3 4 5*
Constant talking to peers, Shouting out
Interrupting teacher, Non-verbal noises
Tapping

22) Movement about the class *1 2 3 4 5*
Wandering about, moving around on the mat
Interfering with others, Leaving the room

23) Public areas *1 2 3 4 5*
Corridors, Playground, Assembly, Toilets, Office
Physical / Verbal aggression to staff / pupils
Intentional / unintentional interference of others
Noise, Misuse of equipment, Graffiti, Litter

24) How does the pupil's behaviour compare with others in the class?

Much worse	*Worse*	*Average*	*Better*	*Much Better*
1	**2**	**3**	**4**	**5**

Please indicate any areas of strength or improvements made recently:

Please indicate two areas that you are concerned about:

Please indicate any strategies you have found useful:

From **Assessing Individual Needs** – H. Ayers, D. Clarke and A. Ross – *David Fulton Publishers – 1996*

Secondary Score Sheet

Name	MATHS	ENGLISH	SCIENCE	TECHNOLOGY	HISTORY	GEOGRAPHY	LANGUAGES	R.E.	P.E. / GAMES	ART	MUSIC				1s or 2s
1 Attendance															
2 Punctuality															
3 Standard of work															
4 Starting work															
5 Work															
6 Cooperation															
7 Independence															
8 Organisation															
9 Work difficulties															
10 Self-confidence															
11 Awareness of others															
12 Self-awareness															
13 Instructions															
14 Friendship															
15 Correction															
16 Disagreements															
17 Playground															
18 Interaction with peers															
19 Interaction with adults															
20 Use of equipment															
21 Pupil noise															
22 Movement															
23 Public areas															
24 Pupil / class															
1s or 2s															

From **Assessing Individual Needs** – H. Ayers, D. Clarke and A. Ross – *David Fulton Publishers – 1996*

SEN Class Monitoring Sheet

Name \ Date:							

B - Behaviour   W - Work   Ab - Absenteeism   Wd - Withdrawn   N - Neglect
Ph - Physical   H - High achievement   I - Improvement   P - Playground
PR - Pupil Relationships   SR - Staff Relationships   Au - Aural   V - Visual   E2L

From **Assessing Individual Needs** – H. Ayers, D. Clarke and A. Ross   –   *David Fulton Publishers – 1996*

Planning Sheet

Describe the main difficulties causing concern as specifically as possible:

1)

2)

Are there other areas causing concern?

Possible contributory factors

Immediate

Background

How do staff respond?

How do other pupils respond?

What other things happen to / are avoided by the pupil?

How might these factors be reinforcing the learning difficulty / behaviour?

What strengths does the pupil have?

Have you considered the 'context issues'? If so how might these be relevant?

From **Assessing Individual Needs** – H. Ayers, D. Clarke and A. Ross   –   *David Fulton Publishers – 1996*

Describe the overall aim of any intervention to be made

What areas are to be the focus of the intervention

What is the initial strategy to be tried?

Date for initial review

Review of initial strategy

Has the duration been reduced?

Has the frequency been reduced?

Has the intensity been reduced?

What is the next strategy to be tried?

Date for review

Review of intervention

Continue on extention sheet if necessary

From **Assessing Individual Needs** – H. Ayers, D. Clarke and A. Ross – *David Fulton Publishers – 1996*

FIXED INTERVAL SAMPLING

Pupil

Class

No. in class

Date

Activity

Class Behaviour Rating -2 -1 0 +1 +2

Setting

Observer

	00	15	30	45	00	15	30	45	00	15	30	45	00	15	30	45

(1) On Task	(2) Talking	(3) Looking	(4) Physical Movement	(5) Fidgeting	(6) Noise	(7) Other	(8)

From **Assessing Individual Needs** – H. Ayers, D. Clarke and A. Ross – *David Fulton Publishers – 1996*

FREQUENCY COUNT SHEET

Date

									BEHAVIOUR
									FREQUENCY

From **Assessing Individual Needs** – H. Ayers, D. Clarke and A. Ross – *David Fulton Publishers – 1996*

ABC OF BEHAVIOUR

	ANTECEDENTS Background	ANTECEDENTS Immediate	BEHAVIOUR	CONSEQUENCES	GENERAL AIM	INTERVENTION

From **Assessing Individual Needs** – H. Ayers, D. Clarke and A. Ross – *David Fulton Publishers – 1996*

PUPIL OBSERVATION SHEET – IEP

Date

PUPIL

CLASS / FORM

TEACHER

SUBJECT

This sheet records behaviours exhibited by a pupil during a lesson

Please ring the appropriate number against each behaviour.
0 = Pupil exhibits this behaviour either NOT AT ALL or NO MORE THAN MOST OTHER PUPILS
1 = This behaviour CAUSES SOME CONCERN
2 = This behaviour CAUSES A LOT OF CONCERN either because of seriousness or frequency

Throws objects	0	1	2	**Damages objects**	0	1	2
Makes noises	0	1	2	**Eats / drinks in classroom**	0	1	2
Interferes with others	0	1	2	**Verbally abuses others**	0	1	2
Physically attacks others	0	1	2	**Refuses to follow instructions**	0	1	2
Fails to bring equipment	0	1	2	**Fails to do enough work**	0	1	2
Calls out	0	1	2	**Chatters**	0	1	2
Arrives late	0	1	2	**Fidgets**	0	1	2
Moves from seat	0	1	2	**Leaves classroom**	0	1	2

TEACHER COMMENTS:

From **Assessing Individual Needs** – H. Ayers, D. Clarke and A. Ross – *David Fulton Publishers* – 1996

IEP INTERVIEW – *Pupil*

PUPIL _____ **INTERVIEWER** _____

Date and time of interview _____

PUNCTUALITY

1) Are you ON TIME: a) For school?   *Rarely*   *Sometimes*   *Usually*

                          a) For lessons?   *Rarely*   *Sometimes*   *Usually*

ATTENDANCE

2) How OFTEN do you come: a) To school?   *Rarely*   *Sometimes*   *Usually*

                               a) To lessons?   *Rarely*   *Sometimes*   *Usually*

LEARNING

3) How good do you think you at:

     a) Concentrating on work?   *Poor*   *Average*   *Good*

     b) Starting work?   *Poor*   *Average*   *Good*

     c) Finishing work?   *Poor*   *Average*   *Good*

     d) Working alone?   *Poor*   *Average*   *Good*

     e) Working with another pupil?   *Poor*   *Average*   *Good*

     f) Working with a group?   *Poor*   *Average*   *Good*

SOCIAL

4) How well do you:

     a) Get on with staff?   *Poor*   *Average*   *Good*

     b) Get on with other pupils?   *Poor*   *Average*   *Good*

     c) Make friends?   *Poor*   *Average*   *Good*

From **Assessing Individual Needs** – H. Ayers, D. Clarke and A. Ross – *David Fulton Publishers – 1996*

SELF-ESTEEM

5) **a) Underline the words you would use to describe YOURSELF:**

Happy	Sad	Good looking	Ugly	Stupid	Clever	Popular
Unpopular	Tough	Weak	Sensible	Lonely	Shy	

b) Underline the words you think PUPILS would use to describe YOU:

Happy	Sad	Good looking	Ugly	Stupid	Clever	Popular
Unpopular	Tough	Weak	Sensible	Lonely	Shy	

c) Underline the words you think TEACHERS would use to describe you:

Happy	Sad	Good looking	Ugly	Stupid	Clever	Popular
Unpopular	Tough	Weak	Sensible	Lonely	Shy	

d) Underline the words you think your PARENTS/CARERS would use to describe you:

Happy	Sad	Good looking	Ugly	Stupid	Clever	Popular
Unpopular	Tough	Weak	Sensible	Lonely	Shy	

BEHAVIOUR TOWARDS OTHER PUPILS

6) **Do you think you are: a) Friendly**

   b) Co-operative

From **Assessing Individual Needs** – H. Ayers, D. Clarke and A. Ross – *David Fulton Publishers – 1996*

IEP INTERVIEW – *Pupil*

BEHAVIOUR TOWARDS TEACHERS

7) Do you think you are:

a) Co-operative	None	Some	Most	All
b) Verbally aggressive	None	Some	Most	All
c) Physically aggressive	None	Some	Most	All
d) Rejecting	None	Some	Most	All
e) Interrupting	None	Some	Most	All

BEHAVIOUR IN CLASS

8) Do you think you:

a) Wander around	None	Some	Most	All
b) Make noise (s)	None	Some	Most	All
c) Misuse equipment	None	Some	Most	All
d) Fail to bring equipment	None	Some	Most	All

BEHAVIOUR IN PUBLIC AREAS

9)

Have you written graffiti:	Corridors	Playground	Toilets	Dining Room
Have you damaged property:	Corridors	Playground	Toilets	Dining Room
Have you bullied other pupils:	Corridors	Playground	Toilets	Dining Room

BEHAVIOUR AT HOME

10) Underline words you think describe your usual behaviour and feelings:

Sad   Happy   Disobedient   Halpful
Angry   Polite   Sociable   Sensible
Fearful   Lonely   Shy   Calm   Kind

INTERVIEWER'S COMMENTS

From **Assessing Individual Needs** – H. Ayers, D. Clarke and A. Ross – *David Fulton Publishers – 1996*

IEP INTERVIEW – *Parent / Carer*

PUPIL [ ]   **INTERVIEWER** [ ]

Parent / Carer's Name [ ]   **Home Language** [ ]

Date and time of interview [ ]

PUNCTUALITY

1) Is .... on time for school?   *Rarely*   *Sometimes*   *Usually*

ATTENDANCE

2) How OFTEN does........................ go to school?   *Rarely*   *Sometimes*   *Usually*

LEARNING

3) When doing homework, how well do you think .... manages to:

a) Concentrate on work?	*Poor*	*Average*	*Good*
b) Start work?	*Poor*	*Average*	*Good*
c) Finish work?	*Poor*	*Average*	*Good*
d) Work without help?	*Poor*	*Average*	*Good*

SOCIAL

4) How well do you think .... is able to:

a) Get on with staff?	*Concerned*	*OK*	*Very well*
b) Get on with other pupils?	*Concerned*	*OK*	*Very well*
c) Make friends?	*Concerned*	*OK*	*Very well*
d) Get on with parents / carers?	*Concerned*	*OK*	*Very well*
e) Get on with brothers	*Concerned*	*OK*	*Very well*
f) Get on with sisters	*Concerned*	*OK*	*Very well*

From **Assessing Individual Needs** – H. Ayers, D. Clarke and A. Ross – *David Fulton Publishers – 1996*

IEP INTERVIEW – *Parent / Carer*

SELF-ESTEEM

5) Underline the words you think ....would use to describe him / herself

Happy	Sad	Good looking	Ugly	Stupid	Clever	Popular
Unpopular		Tough	Weak	Sensible	Lonely	Shy

RELATIONSHIPS

6) Underline the words you think would describe your relationship with ....

Argumentative	Relaxed	Tense	Happy	Calm	Clever	Improving
Deteriorating	Difficult	Rewarding	Strict	Challenging	Aggressive	

7) Underline the words you think describe ....'s relationship with his / her brothers / sisters.

Argumentative	Relaxed	Tense	Happy	Calm	Clever	Improving
Deteriorating	Difficult	Rewarding	Strict	Challenging	Aggressive	

8) Underline the words you think describe ....'s relationship with his / her teachers

Argumentative	Relaxed	Tense	Happy	Calm	Clever	Improving
Deteriorating	Difficult	Rewarding	Strict	Challenging	Aggressive	

BEHAVIOUR TOWARDS TEACHERS

9) As far as you are aware, do you think .... is:

a) Co-operative	*Poor*	*Average*	*Good*
b) Verbally aggressive	*Poor*	*Average*	*Good*
c) Physically aggressive	*Poor*	*Average*	*Good*
d) Rejecting	*Poor*	*Average*	*Good*
e) Interrupting	*Poor*	*Average*	*Good*

From **Assessing Individual Needs** – H. Ayers, D. Clarke and A. Ross – *David Fulton Publishers – 1996*

IEP INTERVIEW – *Parent / Carer*

BEHAVIOUR AT HOME

10) **Do you think ....'s usual behaviour and feelings at home are:**

a)	Happy	*Concerned*	*OK*	*Very well*
b)	Sad	*Concerned*	*OK*	*Very well*
c)	Disobedient	*Concerned*	*OK*	*Very well*
d)	Helpful	*Concerned*	*OK*	*Very well*
e)	Angry	*Concerned*	*OK*	*Very well*
f)	Sociable	*Concerned*	*OK*	*Very well*
g)	Polite	*Concerned*	*OK*	*Very well*
h)	Sensible	*Concerned*	*OK*	*Very well*
i)	Fearful	*Concerned*	*OK*	*Very well*
j)	Kind	*Concerned*	*OK*	*Very well*
k)	Shy	*Concerned*	*OK*	*Very well*
l)	Lonely	*Concerned*	*OK*	*Very well*
m)	Calm	*Concerned*	*OK*	*Very well*

11) **What are your greatest concerns for .... at school?**

ADDITIONAL COMMENTS / OBSERVATIONS

From **Assessing Individual Needs** – H. Ayers, D. Clarke and A. Ross – *David Fulton Publishers – 1996*

Individual Education Plan (E.B.D.)

SEN Stage 2/3

PUPIL DETAILS

Name | | DoB

Form / Class | | Attendance (%): | | M / F

Home Language | | Ethnicity

ASSESSMENT

Underline relevant *italicised* words. Add others where appropriate.

ASSESSMENT INSTRUMENTS *eg: Observation – formal / informal   Checklist   Rating Scale.*
Self-monitoring form   School reports / forms / medicals   Questionnaires   Interviews
ASSESSORS *eg: Parents / Carers   Teachers / other staff   Pupils   External agencies*
CONTEXTS *eg: Classroom   Playground   Corridors   Gym   Assembly   Toilets   Office*

ASSESSMENT SUMMARY: Specific description of main difficulties

FORMULATION

Underline relevant *italicised* words. Add others where appropriate.

FORMULATION: eg Functional analysis using ABC model
State reasons WHY the difficulties occur taking into consideration eg:

Home background   Teaching styles   Teaching materials / methods   Learning styles

Learning difficulties   Classroom management techniques   Whole school factors

'Within - pupil factors'   Medical reasons   Attributions   Lack of appropriate social skills

Underline relevant *italicised* words. Add others where appropriate.

State SPECIFIC TARGETS in POSITIVE TERMS

1) -

2) -

3) -

4) -

State INTERVENTION STRATEGIES   Underline relevant *italicised* words

Positive reinforcement programme   *Monitoring charts*   *Report cards*   *Contracts*
Self-management programme   *Individual / client-centred / behavioural / group counselling*
Circle work   *Time out*   *Token economy*   *Social skills training*   *Assertiveness training*
Peer-tutoring   *Classroom management skills*   *Curricular differentiation*
Literacy / Numeracy / Language programme etc
Other:

NAME those involved with the INTERVENTION (use initials)
Parents / Carers   *Teachers / Other staff*   *Other pupils*   *Governors*   *External agencies etc*

AGREE the duration of the INTERVENTION eg: *Days / Weeks / Terms(s)*
Establish START DATE: Establish REVIEW DATE:

EVALUATION   Underline relevant *italicised* words

COMPARE the behaviour of the pupil BEFORE and AFTER the intervention
Use ASSESSMENT METHODS that were employed originally and include assessments
undertaken by: *Parents / Carers*   *Teachers / other staff*   *Pupils*   *External agencies.*
SUMMARIZE review:

From **Assessing Individual Needs** – H. Ayers, D. Clarke and A. Ross – *David Fulton Publishers – 1996*

Individual Education Plan (Literacy) *SEN Stage 2/3*

PUPIL DETAILS Name [ ] DoB [ ]

Form / Class [ ] Attendance (%): [ ] M / F

Home Language [ ] Ethnicity [ ]

ASSESSMENT Underline relevant *italicised* words. Add others where appropriate.

ASSESSMENT INSTRUMENTS *eg: Sampling – Informal / Running record / Miscue analysis*

Standardised reading test *NC Level descriptors* *SATs* *Reading scales*

Standardised diction test *Interviews*

ASSESSORS *eg: Parents / Carers* *Teachers / other staff* *External agencies*

ASSESSMENT SUMMARY: Specific description of main difficulties

FORMULATION Underline relevant *italicised* words. Add others where appropriate.

FORMULATION: eg Functional analysis using ABC model
State reasons WHY the difficulties occur taking into consideration eg:

Teaching materials / methods *Learning styles* *Emotional factors* *Medical reasons*

Self-image *Family factors* *Specific difficulties* *Phonological awareness*

From **Assessing Individual Needs** – H. Ayers, D. Clarke and A. Ross – *David Fulton Publishers – 1996*

INTERVENTION
Underline relevant *italicised* words. Add others where appropriate.

State SPECIFIC TARGETS in POSITIVE TERMS

1) -

2) -

3) -

4) -

State INTERVENTION STRATEGIES   Underline relevant *italicised* words

Structured reading programme   *Extended choice of material*   *Curricular differentiation*
Home-school literacy initiative   *Word bank / word book programme*   *Spelling programme*
Peer-tutoring   *Paired reading programme*   *Precision teaching programme*   *DISTAR*
Reading recovery programme

NAME those involved with the INTERVENTION (use initials)
Parents / Carers   *Teachers / Other staff*   *Other pupils*   *External agencies etc*

AGREE the duration of the INTERVENTION eg: *Days / Weeks / Terms(s)*
Establish START DATE: Establish REVIEW DATE:

EVALUATION

COMPARE the behaviour of the pupil BEFORE and AFTER the intervention
Use ASSESSMENT METHODS that were employed originally and include assessments
undertaken by: *Parents / Carers*   *Teachers / other staff*   *Pupils*   *External agencies.*
SUMMARIZE review:

From **Assessing Individual Needs** – H. Ayers, D. Clarke and A. Ross – *David Fulton Publishers - 1996*

Primary Assessment Profile

Pupil _____ E2L Stage: **1 2 3 4** Date _____

Class _____ N C Year ____ Home Language _____

Gender **M / F** Medical _____ Teacher _____

Please consider the child's behaviour and learning over the past month and then circle a number (1 - 5) on each continuum (eg Poor - Excellent) where you assess the pupil generally to be.
Please underline any of the example words, or if you want, add any of your own, which describe or indicate the areas of the pupil's difficulties or abilities.

1) Punctuality
1　　2　　3　　4　　5
Poor　　　Acceptable　　　Excellent

2) Attendance
1　　2　　3　　4　　5
Poor　　　Acceptable　　　Excellent

3) Reading Skills
1　　2　　3　　4　　5
Poor　　　Acceptable　　　Excellent

(1) Beginner, (2) Non-fluent, (3) Moderately fluent,
(4) Fluent, (5) Exceptionally fluent

4) Writing
1　　2　　3　　4　　5
Poor　　　Acceptable　　　Excellent

Strings of letters / Awareness of word boundaries / Uses simple phrases repetitively / Writes full sentences / Makes independent attempts at words / Drafting / Independent or fluent writer, Neatness, Legibility

5) Mathematical Skills
1　　2　　3　　4　　5
Poor　　　Acceptable　　　Excellent

Operations $+ - \times \div$, Number bonds, Sorting / Matching, Measurement, Shape and space

6) Artistic / Creative Skills
1　　2　　3　　4　　5
Poor　　　Acceptable　　　Excellent

Visual, Dramatic, Music, Written

7) Practical Skills
1　　2　　3　　4　　5
Poor　　　Acceptable　　　Excellent

Fine work, Using tools and equipment

8) Physical Skills
1　　2　　3　　4　　5
Poor　　　Acceptable　　　Excellent

PE and Games, General coordination

9) Learning Skills
1　　2　　3　　4　　5
Poor　　　Acceptable　　　Excellent

Concentration, Memory, Making connections between ideas, Individual work, Group work, Collaborative work, Distinguishing between class situations and 1-1 situations with teacher, Starting work, Finishing work

10) Communication and Social Skills
1　　2　　3　　4　　5
Poor　　　Acceptable　　　Excellent

Communication with adults, Communication with peers, Leadership skills, Isolated, Unwilling to join in, Making friends, Working with others

P.T.O.

From **Assessing Individual Needs** – H. Ayers, D. Clarke and A. Ross – *David Fulton Publishers* – 1996

11) Attitude towards self

1	2	3	4	5
Poor		Acceptable		Excellent

Blames self, Seems to feel incapable, Poor self-image, Seems unhappy / tearful, Withdrawn, Depressed, Makes negative statements about self, Over-confident, Self-satisfied

12) Attitude towards work

1	2	3	4	5
Poor		Acceptable		Excellent

Reluctant to start, Poor presentation, Unfinished work, Destroys or damages work

13) Attitude towards school

1	2	3	4	5
Poor		Acceptable		Excellent

Destruction of property, Graffiti, Truanting

14) Use of equipment and furniture

1	2	3	4	5
Poor		Acceptable		Excellent

Misuse of equipment, furniture or materials, Failure to bring correct equipment

15) Behaviour towards other pupils

1	2	3	4	5
Poor		Acceptable		Excellent

Physically aggressive, Verbally aggressive, Provoking, Distracting, Damages other's work

16) Behaviour towards staff

1	2	3	4	5
Poor		Acceptable		Excellent

Teaching staff / Non-teaching staff
Physically aggressive, Verbally aggressive, Uncooperative, Cheeky, Undermines authority, Response to commands, Response to reprimands, Specific groups

17) Movement about the class

1	2	3	4	5
Poor		Acceptable		Excellent

Wandering about, interfering with others, leaving classroom

18) Pupil noise

1	2	3	4	5
Poor		Acceptable		Excellent

Constant talking to peers, Shouting out, Interrupting teacher, Non-verbal noises, banging, tapping etc
Volume, Frequency, Duration

19) Public Areas

1	2	3	4	5
Poor		Acceptable		Excellent

Corridors / Playground / Assembly / Toilets / Office
Physical / Verbal aggression to staff / Pupils, Intentional / unintentional interference with others,
Lining-up, Inappropriate movement, Inappropriate noise
Mistreatment of equipment or furniture, Graffiti, Litter

20) How does the pupil's behaviour compare with others in the class?

1	2	3	4	5
Worse		Average		Better

Please prioritise and briefly describe 2 areas of particular concern:

No. ( )

No. ( )

Other comments (including positive observations):

Please return to:	By:

Thank you for your cooperation.

From **Assessing Individual Needs** – H. Ayers, D. Clarke and A. Ross – *David Fulton Publishers – 1996*

Secondary Assessment Profile

Pupil [ ]   E2L Stage: **I 2 3 4**   Date [/ /]

Form [ ]   N C Year [ ]   Subject [ ]

Gender [M / F]   Medical [ ]   Teacher [ ]

Please consider the child's behaviour and learning over the past month and then circle a number (1 - 5) on each continuum (eg Poor - Excellent) where you assess the pupil generally to be.
<u>Please underline any of the example words</u>, or if you want, add any of your own, which describe or indicate the areas of the pupil's difficulties or abilities.

1) Punctuality
1   2   3   4   5
Poor   Acceptable   Excellent

2) Attendance
1   2   3   4   5
Poor   Acceptable   Excellent

3) Reading Skills
1   2   3   4   5
Poor   Acceptable   Excellent

(1) Beginner, (2) Non-fluent, (3) Moderately fluent,
(4) Fluent, (5) Exceptionally fluent

4) Writing
1   2   3   4   5
Poor   Acceptable   Excellent

Illegible, Untidy presentation, Non-fluent

5) Mathematical Skills
1   2   3   4   5
Poor   Acceptable   Excellent

Operations + - × ÷ , Tables, Using a calculator,
Decimals, Explorations

6) Artistic / Creative Skills
1   2   3   4   5
Poor   Acceptable   Excellent

Visual, Dramatic, Music, Written

7) Practical Skills
1   2   3   4   5
Poor   Acceptable   Excellent

Fine work, Using tools and equipment

8) Physical Skills
1   2   3   4   5
Poor   Acceptable   Excellent

PE and Games, General coordination

9) Learning Skills
1   2   3   4   5
Poor   Acceptable   Excellent

Concentration, Memory, Making connections between
ideas, Individual work, Group work, Collaborative work,
Distinguishing between class situations and 1 – 1 situations
with teacher, Starting work, Finishing work

10) Communication and Social Skills
1   2   3   4   5
Poor   Acceptable   Excellent

Communication with adults, Communication with peers,
Leadership skills, Isolated, Unwilling to join in,
Making friends, Working with others

P.T.O.

From **Assessing Individual Needs** – H. Ayers, D. Clarke and A. Ross – *David Fulton Publishers – 1996*

11) Attitude towards self

1   2   3   4   5

Poor   Acceptable   Excellent

Blames self, Seems to feel incapable, Poor self-image, Seems unhappy / tearful, Withdrawn, Depressed, Makes negative statements about self, Over-confident, Self-satisfied

12) Attitude towards work

1   2   3   4   5

Poor   Acceptable   Excellent

Reluctant to start, Poor presentation, Unfinished work, Destroys or damages work

13) Attitude towards school

1   2   3   4   5

Poor   Acceptable   Excellent

Destruction of property, Graffiti, Truanting

14) Use of equipment and furniture

1   2   3   4   5

Poor   Acceptable   Excellent

Misuse of equipment, furniture or materials, Failure to bring correct equipment

15) Behaviour towards other pupils

1   2   3   4   5

Poor   Acceptable   Excellent

Physically aggressive, Verbally aggressive, Provoking, Distracting, Damages other's work

16) Behaviour towards staff

1   2   3   4   5

Poor   Acceptable   Excellent

Teaching staff / Non-teaching staff
Physically aggressive, Verbally aggressive, Uncooperative, Cheeky, Undermines authority, Response to commands, Response to reprimands, Specific groups

17) Movement about the class

1   2   3   4   5

Poor   Acceptable   Excellent

Wandering about, interfering with others, leaving classroom

18) Pupil noise

1   2   3   4   5

Poor   Acceptable   Excellent

Constant talking to peers, Shouting out, Interrupting teacher, Non-verbal noises, banging, tapping etc Volume, Frequency, Duration

19) Public Areas

1   2   3   4   5

Poor   Acceptable   Excellent

Corridors / Playground / Assembly / Toilets / Office
Physical / Verbal aggression to staff / Pupils, Intentional / unintentional interference with others,
Lining-up, Inappropriate movement, Inappropriate noise
Mistreatment of equipment or furniture, Graffiti, Litter

20) How does the pupil's behaviour compare with others in the class?

1   2   3   4   5

Worse   Average   Better

Please prioritise and briefly describe 2 areas of particular concern:

No. (   )

No. (   )

Other comments (including positive observations):

Secondary Assessment Profile Score Sheet

Name: _____   Date: _____   Sheet no. ____

Column headers (subjects):
MATHS, ENGLISH, SCIENCE, TECHNOLOGY, GEOGRAPHY, HISTORY, ART, LANGUAGES, MUSIC, P.E. / GAMES, R.E.

Row categories:
1 Punctuality
2 Attendance
3 Reading
4 Writing
5 Maths
6 Artistic
7 Practical
8 Physical
9 Learning
10 Social
11 Self
12 Work
13 School
14 Equipment
15 Pupils
16 Staff
17 Movement
18 Noise
19 Public Areas
20 Pupil-Class

Score columns: 1's, 2's, 3's, 4's, 5's

Designed and Produced by the Don Clarke and Harry Ayers

From **Assessing Individual Needs** – H. Ayers, D. Clarke and A. Ross – *David Fulton Publishers – 1996*

BIBLIOGRAPHY

Ayers, H., Clarke., Murray, A., (1995) *Perspectives on Behaviour.* London: David Fulton Publishers.

Ainscow M. (1991) *Effective Schools For All,* London, David Fulton Publishers.

Burns, R.B. (1979) *The Self Concept,* London: Longman

Caspari, Irene, (1976) *Troublesome Children in the Classroom,* London: Routledge

Cooper, P. (1995) *Helping Them To Learn,* Stafford: NASEN

Department of Education and Science (DES) (1989) *Discipline in Schools, Report of the Committee of Enquiry chaired by Lord Elton,* London, HMSO.

DfE, (1994) *Pupils with Problems,* HMSO

Fontana, David, (1981) *Psychology for Teachers,* BPS Books, Macmillan

Galloway, D., Armstrong, P., Tomlinson, S., (1994) *The Assessment of Special Educational Needs: Whose Problem?* Harlow: Longmans

Gipps, C. and Stobart, G. (1993) *Assessment: A Teachers' Guide to the Issues,* London: Hodder & Stoughton.

Hanko, G. (1985) *Special Needs in Ordinary Classrooms: An Approach to Teacher Support and Pupil Care,* Oxford, Blackwell.

Leach, D J and Reybould, E C. (1977) *Learning and Behaviour Difficulties in School,* London: Open Books

McManus. M. (1990) Troublesome Behaviour in the Classroom. A Teachers' Survival Guide, Routledge.

Mongon, D. and Hart , S. (1989) *Improving Classroom Behaviour: New Directions for Teachers and Pupils,* London: Cassell.

Norwich, B. (1990) *Reappraising Special Needs Education,* London: Cassell

Ollendick, T.H. and Hersen, M. (1984) *Child Behavioural Assessment: Principles and Procedures,* Oxford: Pergamon Press.

Pearson, L. and Lindsay, G. (1986) *Special Needs in the Ordinary School,* NFER-Nelson

Robertson, John, (1989) (Second Edition) *Effective Classroom Control,* Hodder & Stoughton

Rogers, Bill, (1994) *Behaviour Recovery,* Australia: ACER

Saltzberger-Wittenberg, Esca, (1993) T*he Emotional Experience of Teaching and Learning,* Routledge

Wheldall, K., Merrett, F., and Glynn, T., (1986) *Behaviour Analysis in Educational Psychology:* In Association with Positive Products. Beckenham: Croom Helm.

Sheldon, B. (1982) *Behaviour Modification: Theory, Practice and Philosophy,* Tavistock Publications.

Stow and Self (1989) *Understanding Children with Special Needs,* Hyman

Varma, V.P. (1993) *Management of Behaviour in Schools,* Harlow: Longman.

Westmacott and Cameron, (1981) *Behaviour Can Change,* MacMillan Education

Wolfendale, S., (1993) Assessing Special Educational Needs, London: Cassell